CAE

PRACTICE
— TESTS —

Five tests for the
Cambridge Certificate in
Advanced English

MARK HARRISON • ROSALIE KERR

WITH ANSWERS

Oxford University Press
Walton Street
Oxford OX2 6DP

Oxford   New York   Toronto   Madrid   Delhi   Bombay
Calcutta   Madras   Karachi   Kuala Lumpur
Singapore   Hong Kong   Nairobi   Dar es Salaam
Cape Town   Melbourne   Auckland

and associated companies in
Berlin   Ibadan

OXFORD and OXFORD ENGLISH
are trade marks of Oxford University Press

ISBN 0 19 4533409
ISBN 0 19 4533417 (With Answers edition)
© Oxford University Press 1994

Typeset by Tradespools Limited, Frome, Somerset
Printed in Hong Kong

Acknowledgements

*The authors and publisher are grateful to those who have given permission to
reproduce the following extracts and adaptations of copyright material:*

pp 6-7 four reviews from *TVTimes*, IPC Magazines Ltd. pp 8-10 from
the *Hendon and Finchley Times*. p 10 'Wing Tips' from *ES*, ©*ES*/Solo.
p 12 by David Lister from *The Independent*. p 16 from M Sheldon:
Orwell - The Authorized Biography, (Wm. Heinemann Ltd, 1991),
Reed International Books. p 18 from 'Suspension of Belief' by John
Collee in *The Observer Magazine*, Peters Frazer and Dunlop Group
Ltd. p 19 from 'Towards a global language' by Tony Scarfi from the
Education Guardian, ©The Guardian. p 21 from 'One happy island' by
Peter Fairley, *Country House And Interiors*, and Peter Fairley. p 29 from
'Give your memory a going-over' *SHE*/Rita Carter. pp 31-2 from *The
Observer* ©. pp 34-5 'Open wide and trust me, this won't hurt!'
Women's Own. p 36 adapted from articles by John Illman and Jim
Horne from *The Guardian*, © The Guardian. p 40 'Guarding the
change at the palace' by Juliet Solomon from *Northbound*. p 42 by
Thomas Delclos from *Expo 92 Supplement, The Independent*. p 43 from
M Pritchard: *Let's Go Fishing* (Octopus, 1985), Reed International
Books. p 45 'Staying warm but keeping cool', ©*Daily Mail*/Solo. pp
54-5 'From small acorns...' by Tessa Nicholson from *AA Magazine*,
1992, HHL. p 56 from The Linda Gillard Column, *Ideal Home*, Linda
Gillard. p 59 by Paul Wolstencroft of Barfield Enterprise Training. p
60 by Michael White from *The Independent on Sunday*. p 64 adapted
extracts from Hugh Brogan: *Longman History of the United States*,
(1985), (paperback edition entitled *The Penguin History of the USA)*,
Longman Group UK Ltd. p 66 from *HELLO!* Copyright Hello!
Magazine 1992. p 69 from *BEST*, Copyright best magazine 1992,
Gruner & Jahr (UK). p 77 'How to you doodle' by Gloria Hargreaves
from *BEST*, Copyright best magazine 1992 Gruner & Jahr (UK). pp
80-1 from 'Working in Agriculture and Horticulture', the Careers and
Occupational Information Centre, Sheffield. pp 82-3 'World where
inflation is a lot of hot air' by David Hunn from *The Sunday Times*,
David Hunn. p 89 'If all else fails, read the instructions' by Karen
Gold, from *New*

Scientist. p 91 from *The Observer* ©. p 94 from David Parlett: *The
Penguin Book of Card Games*, (Allen Lane 1979), Copyright © David
Parlett, 1978. p 99 taped interview from *Conversation Piece*, (BBC
Radio 4, 29.3.92), Sir Ranulph Fiennes and the BBC. p 105 from
Good Housekeeping Magazine. pp 106-7 Code of Practice, the Press
Standards Board of Finance Ltd. p 109 'In a rut' by Georgina Gold,
Living Magazine. p 113 'Is your body clock running on time? by Isabel
Walker, *Living Magazine*. p 115 from J. Healy: *The Grass Arena*
(Faber, 1988) John Healy. p 116 from Dee Brown: *Bury My Heart at
Wounded Knee*, (Vintage, 1970), The Peters Frazer & Dunlop Group
Ltd.

*Although every effort has been made to trace and contact copyright holders
before publication, we have not been able to do so for the following items. We
apologize for any apparent infringement of copyright and if notified, the
publisher will be pleased to rectify these omissions at the earliest opportunity.*

P 67 from an article by Christopher Lloyd in *The Sunday Times*.
p 85 from 'Beliefs about bees' buy Paul Prossart in *The Lady*.
p 92 from A Lipsanen: *The Finnish Folk Year* (Otava 1987).
P 102-3 Record Sleeve notes by Lawrence Cohn.

The authors and publisher are grateful to the University of Cambridge
Local Examinations Syndicate *for permission to reproduce the sample
answer sheets on pages 126-130, and the information on page 149 in the
With Answers edition.*

The authors and publishers are especially grateful to Howard Booth *for
permission to use his photographs in this book.*

*The publisher would also like to thank the following for their permission to
reproduce photographs:*

Mike Dudley; Halifax Building Society/DFSD Bozell; Houses and
Interiors Photographic agency; Impact Photos; The Telegraph Colour
Library; Elizabeth Whiting and Associates.

Illustrations by:
Caroline Bays; Oxford Illustrators.

*The tests were piloted with several groups of students preparing for CAE. The
following teachers and their students deserve special thanks:*
Nathan Brown, International Language Academy, London; Helen
Gialias and Norma Innes, Anglo-Continental School of English,
Bournemouth; Ken Griffiths, The British School, Trieste; Clare
McGinn, King Street College, London; James Roy, Oxford Academy,
Oxford; Katy Shaw, Lewisham College, London.

The sample student answers were provided by:
Cecilia Åkerdahl of International Language Academy; Marie-Ange
Jean Baptiste and Andrea Bauer of Lewisham College; Lorena
Mendoza of Oxford Academy; Magdelena Zacikiewicz of King Street
College.

CONTENTS

INTRODUCTION

This book contains five complete practice tests for the Cambridge Certificate in Advanced English (CAE). Developed by experienced CAE item writers, the tests accurately reflect the coverage of the real examination. Great care has been taken to include the many different formats and question types of each paper, and the tests as a group offer a full range of practice for the CAE.

The CAE

Note: In Papers 1, 3 and 4, candidates have to write their answers on special answer sheets. See pages 126–130 for examples of these.

PAPER 1   READING   (1 hour + 15 minutes)

In this paper, candidates are expected to answer approximately 40–45 questions on four different texts in one hour. They then have 15 minutes to transfer their answers to the special answer sheet. The four texts are taken from authentic sources such as newspapers, magazines and a variety of non-fiction material. In this book, the twenty reading texts have each come from a different source, to give the student a wide exposure to possible examination text types.

The complete reading paper consists of one double page text using a multiple matching test format, usually with between 15 and 20 questions; one shorter text and multiple matching task; one gapped text where candidates have to fit up to 8 paragraphs into the gaps; one text followed by usually between 5 and 8 multiple choice questions.

PAPER 2   WRITING   (2 hours)

This paper has two sections of equal importance. All candidates must answer Question 1 in Section A. In this question, candidates first read up to 400 words of written material in the form of short extracts, which provide the context and information for their answer. They then write a total of about 250 words, which may be made up of one or more written tasks, for example a formal note and an informal letter. Section B offers candidates a choice of four different writing tasks, including text types such as reports, articles, letters, etc., each of which must be about 250 words in length.

PAPER 3   ENGLISH IN USE   (1 hour 30 minutes)

The authentic texts in this paper have each come from a different source. There are three sections to the paper, with a total of 6 separate questions. Section A contains two 'cloze' passages: Question 1 consists of a gapped

passage and 15 multiple choice questions testing vocabulary; Question 2 presents a short passage with 15 gaps into which candidates must insert one grammatically correct word. Section B tests editing skills in Question 3, which involves the correction of errors in a short text, and an awareness of register and style in Question 4, where candidates have to transfer information from one written style to another, for example from informal to formal, or from formal to informal. Section C has two different tasks: Question 5 entails deciding which phrases or short sentences fit into gaps in a text; Question 6 involves writing sentences about a subject from given notes.

PAPER 4   LISTENING   (approximately 45 minutes)

Candidates are given 10 minutes at the end of this paper to transfer their answers to an answer sheet. The paper has four sections. In Section A candidates will hear one person talking and are required to write down information given by the speaker. The recording will be heard twice. Section B is a similar task, but the recording will only be heard once. In Section C candidates will hear more than one speaker, in recordings such as interviews and simulated radio broadcasts, and are required to demonstrate an understanding of content, with special emphasis on the attitudes or opinions of the speakers. The recording will be heard twice. Section D comprises five short extracts of different people speaking, and candidates have to do two separate tasks, identifying for example speaker, subject, purpose, attitude, etc. The recording will be heard twice.

PAPER 5   SPEAKING   (approximately 15 minutes)

Candidates do this part of the examination in pairs, or sometimes in a group of three. There are two examiners present. There is an introductory phase (A), during which candidates ask and answer questions on personal matters. In Phase B, they take turns at doing tasks based on photographs or other visual materials. Tasks normally involve an information gap. Phase C requires the candidates to work collaboratively, discussing a problem and arriving at an agreement, or agreeing to disagree. The final phase (D) consists of further discussion arising from the topic of Phase C. Candidates may be required to explain each other's opinions as well as their own.

For further information about the CAE, write to:
  EFL Section
  University of Cambridge Local Examinations Syndicate
  1 Hills Road
  Cambridge CB1 2EU
  UK

PAPER 1   READING   (1 HOUR + 15 MINUTES)

FIRST TEXT/QUESTIONS 1–19

Answer questions *1–19* by referring to the film reviews on pages *6–7*. Indicate your answers **on the separate answer sheet**.

Questions *1–12*. According to the reviews, on which day or days can you see a film of which the following statements are true? Choose your answers from the list of days **A–G**. You may choose any of the days more than once.

There is some excellent acting in it.	1	2	A	Saturday
It moves along rather slowly.	3		B	Sunday
It has good pictures of scenery.	4		C	Monday
The story is difficult to follow.	5	6	D	Tuesday
It will keep you in a state of tension.	7	8	E	Wednesday
Many people dislike it.	9		F	Thursday
It is a peculiar film.	10	11	G	Friday
It starts with a lot of action.	12			

For questions *13–19*, look at the list of questions below and choose which of the films from list **A–J** answers each question. You will need to choose some of the films more than once.

Which films are based on true stories?	A	HERO AT LARGE
13 ....14	B	AUNTIE MAME
Which film features someone who later played bigger parts?	C	EDUCATING RITA
15	D	CROSS CREEK
Which films were originally a book or play?	E	SPECIAL DELIVERY
16 ....17 ....18	F	NOBODY RUNS FOREVER
Which film made its leading actress famous?	G	FALLEN ANGEL
19	H	SINK OR SWIM
	I	DESIREE
	J	PRIZZI'S HONOUR

Remember to put your answers on the separate answer sheet.

THIS WEEK'S FILMS ON TV

SATURDAY

Henna

A young man is all ready for his wedding when a storm sweeps him away to sea and he wakes up in the care of a young girl. He finds that he has no memory of his past life. He falls in love with the girl but a storm on their wedding night brings back his memory and he realises that he must go back home. The film is put together with considerable charm.

Auntie Mame

A straight comedy version of the musical but without its vitality. Rosalind Russell recreates her stage role as the ultra-confident, eccentric aunt who adopts a young orphan.

Prizzi's Honour

A comedy based on Richard Condon's novel, with Jack Nicholson as a murderer up to his neck in danger and romance when he meets the mysterious Katheleen Turner. The stars are on great form, with Nicholson at his best and Turner all ice-cold beauty and intelligence. The very complex tale includes an excessively jealous ex-girlfriend. This was a big hit and it's a treat – but be warned: it's a movie with as many enemies as admirers.

SUNDAY

Lonely Hearts

Affectionate, odd and funny tale about a 50-year-old man who starts finding out about women after his over-protective mother dies. He decides to splash out on an introduction through a lonely hearts club and meets the delightful but painfully shy Patricia. However, things don't go as smoothly as he had hoped.

Hero at Large

Out-of-work actor Steve Nichols earns rent money by making public appearances as cartoon character Captain Avenger. On the way home from an appearance (and still in costume) he finds himself foiling a robbery and becoming a hero for real, making everyone think there really is a Captain Avenger. Future leading man Kevin Bacon has a small role.

MONDAY

Fallen Angel

Dana Andrews drifts into a small Californian town with only a dollar to his name. Instantly he falls for waitress Linda Darnell, but she's only interested in men with money. So he decides that the best way to get some is to marry rich, shy, Alice Faye and then divorce her. But he becomes the prime suspect for murder. A stylish movie with a good plot.

Desiree

Director Henry Koster was more at home with comedy and musicals and it shows in his handling of this historical drama. He's not helped by a rather dull script, which tells of the relationship between an Emperor and the daughter of a silk merchant. Fact is liberally mixed with fiction and it affords Marlon Brando, who adopts an uncomfortable tone of voice, few chances to do much other than to wear a succession of uniforms.

I Know Where I'm Going

A romantic drama with some originality, as you might expect from the film-making team of Michael Powell and Emeric Pressburger. Their script abounds in wit, charm and wonderful characters. Most of these are female, including Wendy Hiller as the heroine who thinks she knows where she's going when she heads up to Scotland to marry a millionaire. Nicely shot on location in the Scottish islands.

TUESDAY

Cross Creek
The story of real-life writer Marjorie Kinnan Rawlings, who in 1926 left her husband and home in the big city to start a new life in the Florida backwoods, soaking up the atmosphere in the hope of writing a 'great American novel'. Mary Steenburgen's performance as the sensitive writer is terrific but the film is stronger on character and atmosphere than pace.

Bluffing It
Dennis Weaver is the tough-talking factory foreman who manages to hide his inability to read or write until circumstances force him to face up to the problem. Weaver is OK but it fails to stir the emotions.

Bad Day at Black Rock
The express train doesn't usually stop at the desert town of Black Rock, so when stranger Spencer Tracy steps off it, the moody locals know something is up. The material is good – and very original – and the situations positively crackle with suspense, keeping you on the edge of your seat. There are convincing performances from some of Hollywood's best actors, headed by Tracy as the war veteran who won't give up until he finds out just what guilty secret they've all got to hide.

WEDNESDAY

Special Delivery
An action caper that skilfully steers its way between thriller, romance and black comedy. A breathless opening, when four ex-soldiers rob a bank posing as toy salesmen, gives way to some nice jokes, building to a suspenseful climax that will have you anxious to find out how things turn out.

Malcolm
A pleasantly eccentric comedy about a childlike amateur inventor who takes to bank robbing after losing his job as a mechanic. He meets an ex-criminal who helps him to put his various funny inventions to good criminal use. Good visual jokes but it would have been funnier with a better script.

THURSDAY

Sink or Swim
Handsome Jean-Paul Belmondo plays a fun-loving Frenchman who is all set to marry a mega-rich woman in America's Deep South when a jealous rival reveals a naughty secret from his past.

FRIDAY

Educating Rita
Julie Walters is a hairdresser who longs for a university education and Michael Caine is the tutor who quickly becomes attracted by her loud-mouthed eagerness to learn. Willy Russell's bittersweet comedy proved even more popular on film than on stage and it was the film that established Walters as a major film star.

Nobody Runs Forever
Detective Rod Taylor investigates the suspicious death of the first wife of a diplomat in this ridiculous, complicated adventure. The script is completely lacking in originality and although the actors try hard, the story offers them little help.

SECOND TEXT/QUESTIONS 20–26

*For questions **20–26**, you must choose which of the paragraphs **A–H** on page **9** match the numbered gaps in the magazine article below. There is one extra paragraph which does not belong in any of the gaps. Indicate your answers **on the separate answer sheet**.*

Justin has just the picture

ADVERTISING FEATURE

Having an aptitude for something usually makes a person excel at it.

20

His assignment for his exam, a slide and commentary presentation, was so well received by his tutors that they entered him in a competition organised by a local newspaper … and Justin was the unanimous winner.

21

Justin Grainge Photography is based at Weldon House. The modern, fully equipped studios are on the top floor, where Justin and his team produce work for a large number of companies, ranging from small firms to huge conglomerates.

22

All this further encouraged Justin, who says: "Over the years, people used to ask me if I did portraits and I used to say No. That was because I had regarded myself as a commercial photographer, shooting conferences, presentations and buildings, and doing product shots in a studio."

23

"So we decided to branch out and reorganise the studio to enable me to launch myself as a portrait photographer."

24

This new side of Justin's talent is, however, restricted to evenings and weekends, mainly because he is in such great demand for his commercial work. However, subject to commitments, he can fit in weekday sittings if necessary, so long as the client agrees to the possibility of cancellations if commercial work intervenes.

25

His 10 years' experience in commercial work have given him the patience and talent to put sitters at ease when it comes to portraits … and especially with children.

26

Commercial and portrait photography are both specialist professions which have been mastered by Justin, who has come a long way since his early schooldays and his first little camera.

A   ''It was my mother who eventually pointed out the numerous boardroom pictures I had taken, which, after all, were portraits.''

B   This encouraged him to continue to learn and practise photography, and today, at the age of 26, he is at the top of his profession – a much in demand commercial photographer, and currently expanding his talents into portraiture.

C   Justin will also undertake the commission at the sitter's home, but this would entail an extra charge for the transportation of cameras, lights, backdrop and any other props necessary.

D   This discount applies to the sitting only. Prices of enlargements and choice of frame and material are not included.

E   For Justin Grainge, it has always been photography, ever since his early days at school when, armed with a small camera, he decided to learn the art of taking pictures, rather than join his pals in metal work, carpentry or other traditional classes.

F   It was during this commercial work that Justin found his gift for portrait photography. On numerous occasions, he was required to take pictures of heads of organisations – chairmen, Managing Directors, directors – in the boardroom – and he received numerous commendations in the process.

G   Justin has now re-equipped his modern studio to cater for all types of portraits, and invested in new lights and backdrops. He operates a framing service and offers colour portraits on paper or canvas, mounted on board or blocks, and in any preferred size.

H   In addition to all this, he is an accomplished photographic assessor. He has judged numerous amateur competitions and has also appeared on television, answering viewers' questions and instructing them on how to improve their pictures.

Remember to put your answers on the separate answer sheet.

*Read the following magazine article and then answer the questions on page **11**. Indicate your answers **on the separate answer sheet**.*

TIPS FOR AIR TRAVELLERS

A

Membership of an airline loyalty club will guarantee you a seat on a flight, even when that flight is fully booked for 'normal passengers'. Air France, KLM, Scandinavian Airlines and Singapore Airlines are just four carriers offering this facility to their very best customers. Others, like British Airways, Lufthansa and Swissair, are not quite so bold with their claims but all will move heaven and earth to secure a seat for their club members.

B

First-class and business-class passengers get the pick of the seating, 'up front', away from all the engine noise and vibration. Economy passengers are invariably seated in the noisier, back rows of the aircraft, where the air is usually staler. There are exceptions, however, and airline seating plans (displayed in timetables) enable you to choose the best seat.

C   Cheap excess baggage

Travelling with overweight baggage can cost you dearly. On long-haul flights, the airlines give you a free baggage allowance of between 20 and 64 kilos, depending on the class of travel and the route. Every excess kilo is charged at one per cent of the first-class fare. One way round this is to hand over your baggage to an excess-baggage company, which can save you as much as 70 per cent on airline fees. Your luggage will then travel to your destination unaccompanied, and you can either collect it from the airport or have it delivered to your destination address. It won't usually arrive the same day, though.

D

Booking a first-class or business-class ticket usually entitles you to use the more peaceful airline executive lounge at the airport. Regular passengers with an airline can also use the lounges, even when flying on cut-price economy tickets.

E   Lost luggage compensation

The unthinkable has happened. You have arrived overseas but your luggage has not appeared on the airport baggage carousel. Keep calm. In most cases your bags will turn up, eventually. But, before you leave the airport, contact a member of staff and complete a Baggage Irregularity Report, which ensures that you will receive compensation. However, airlines pay out pitiful compensation, so do read the small print on your ticket, and it's essential to take out adequate insurance beforehand.

F

Securing an upgrade is easier than ever before. Canadian Airlines will now seat some transatlantic passengers who have paid the economy fare in business class, while business-class passengers bound for New York, Toronto, Delhi or Bombay are automatically upgraded to first-class if they have paid the full business-class fare. In addition, large companies are increasingly negotiating an automatic upgrade with airlines.

G   Save on taxi fares

Several airlines are prepared to chauffeur their first-class and business-class passengers to the airport free of charge. These transfers, usually within a 120-kilometre radius, are offered by numerous airlines, including Air Canada, Canadian Airlines, Emirates, Japan's ANA, Northwest, Qantas and Virgin Atlantic. Some carriers will also provide transport on arrival.

H

Taking a companion along and combining business with pleasure costs less than you might think. Many airlines grant a 50 per cent discount for a partner in business class, while a few – Singapore Airlines and JAL, for example – provide two tickets for the price of one, either for use together or at a later date. European fliers staying over a Saturday qualify for excursion fares, which enable two to travel for less than the price of one business-class ticket.

For questions **27–31**, choose the most suitable heading for each of the following sections of the article from the list **A–H** below.

27   Section A

28   Section B

29   Section D

30   Section F

31   Section H

A   Bargain prices

B   The best airlines

C   Ensuring availability

D   Changing to a better seat

E   Advance bookings

F   Escaping the crowds

G   The best times to fly

H   In-flight comfort

For questions **32–38**, answer by choosing from the sections of the article **A–H**.
Note: When more than one answer is required, these may be given **in any order**.
   Some sections may be chosen more than once.

Which section refers to:

passengers who frequently fly on the same airline   **32** ....   **33** ....

ways of avoiding airline rules   **34** ....

variations in the layout of aircraft   **35** ....

checking the airline's legal obligations   **36** ....

promises made by airlines   **37** ....   **38** ....

Remember to put your answers on the separate answer sheet.

*Read the following newspaper article and then answer the questions on page **13**. Indicate your answers **on the separate answer sheet**.*

Art could take pain out of public transport

By David Lister
Arts Correspondent

Travelling on British public transport could become a pleasurable, artistic and educational experience, according to a report.

This could be achieved by simple and inexpensive measures such as information sheets on inter-city journeys detailing sights and monuments; language and 'places to visit' workshops on ferries; children's coaches with videos and storytelling on trains; artwork in airport departure lounges; and poems, photographs and paintings on buses and trains and at bus and railway stations.

The study of the arts in the transport system is fiercely critical about the lack of public art and notes that mostly it is limited to painting.

Naseem Khan and Ken Worpole, the arts policy researchers who wrote the report, conclude that well thought-out and positioned initiatives like Poems on the Underground (posters of poems in tube train carriages) can improve the experience of travel and gain dedicated fans.

Generally, though, hours spent on public transport are "spent in a state that can range from boredom to annoyance. Travelling has become a depressing experience, a state in which one thinks of nothing in order to minimise unpleasantness."

But people who travel abroad bring back memories of Stockholm's metro system, with art in each station reflecting the world above, be it a park or a university, or Melbourne's artist-painted buses.

The authors point out that Britain's transport system used to stir the imagination. Sepia photographs of resorts used to decorate old railway carriages, old London Transport posters encouraged travellers to explore their own city and in the Thirties a travel guide was sold on the London–Penzance express, detailing the route and giving historical information.

Public art, the report says, too often gives the impression of having been slipped in quietly in the hope that it will have been accepted before it has been noticed. The wall designs which decorate the passageways at Heathrow airport are described as "dull and unexciting". But praise is given to the sculptures at Brixton railway station. While the report says that there is no substitute for good architecture and design, some of its most interesting recommendations call for more imaginative developments than just concentrating on the visual arts. "The presence of personal stereos and new technology suggest the introduction of fresh developments such as journey tapes containing information on, or music and poetry related to, the sights being passed."

Live performance carries the danger of being a nuisance, but videos on trains travelling to festivals, containing information on shows, with booking available from train phones, would, says the report, provide a welcome service.

"There is scope for a journey to be turned into a positive experience rather than being merely a passive period to be lived through. Journeys are not among the trials of life but among the opportunities."

39 The researchers concluded that

    A   the public are not interested in art on public transport.

    B   art on public transport should be carefully situated.

    C   art on public transport should be very simple.

    D   paintings are not suitable for public transport.

40 What has changed about art on British transport, according to the report?

    A   It has been copied from the art on foreign transport systems.

    B   It no longer inspires people to visit places.

    C   It no longer provides information about places.

    D   It has been put in different places from in the past.

41 According to the researchers, what is wrong with public art at the moment?

    A   It is in old-fashioned styles.

    B   It irritates the public.

    C   It does not stand out enough.

    D   It does not make travellers relaxed.

42 What should be introduced, according to their report?

    A   musicians playing on public transport

    B   material for travellers to listen to

    C   more paintings on public transport

    D   videos in railway stations

43 The researchers approve of the art on public transport in

    A   Stockholm and Brixton.

    B   Melbourne and Heathrow.

    C   Penzance and Brixton.

    D   Stockholm and Heathrow.

44 Which statement best sums up the researchers' opinions?

    A   On public transport modern art is better than older styles.

    B   Travellers dislike the art they see on British transport.

    C   Art on British transport should be made more striking.

    D   There should be lots of paintings on public transport.

Remember to put your answers on the separate answer sheet.

PAPER 2 WRITING (2 HOURS)

SECTION A

1   A recent holiday on Atlantic Island was spoilt when you suffered from a bad sore throat after
swimming in polluted sea-water. On your return you found some interesting information in a
scientific report.

*Read the publicity material and the extract from the scientific report carefully, and then, **using the
information given**, write the letter described below.*

For **SUN** ... **SAND** ... and clear blue **SEA** ... come to

ATLANTIC ISLAND!

For a relaxing holiday for all the family, you can't do better than let
us welcome you to **ATLANTIC ISLAND**. Our miles of golden sands
are justly famous, and in these environmentally conscious days
you'll be pleased to hear that our sheltered bays don't just look
inviting to swimmers and wind-surfers – our sea-water is just as
clean and pure as it used to be in the days before anyone had even
heard of pollution ...

REPORT ON THE CONDITION OF ATLANTIC ISLAND BEACHES (*contd.*)

and pollution levels were tested on a large sample of the Island's most
popular tourist beaches. Diagram 4.1. shows a marked change in the
situation between 1990 and the present, with the clean beaches
where it is safe to swim being shown as a percentage of the sample:

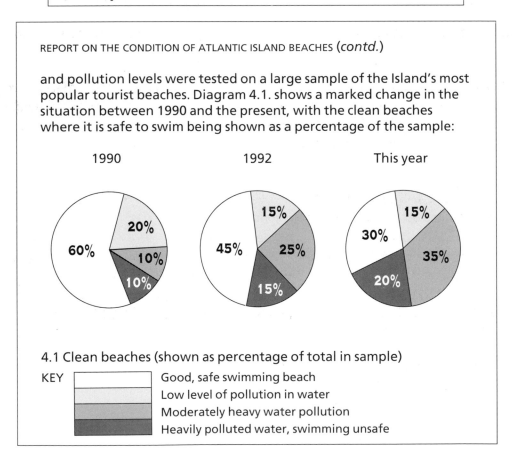

4.1 Clean beaches (shown as percentage of total in sample)

KEY
Good, safe swimming beach
Low level of pollution in water
Moderately heavy water pollution
Heavily polluted water, swimming unsafe

---

*Now write **a letter** to the Atlantic Island Tourist Board, telling them about your experience while on holiday,
and pointing out that their publicity material is misleading. Support your argument with information taken
from the scientific report. You are advised to write approximately 250 words.*

You must lay out your letter in an appropriate way but it is not necessary to include an address.

SECTION B

*Choose **ONE** of the following writing tasks. Your answer should follow exactly the instructions given. Write approximately 250 words.*

2   Your national airline has asked you to write **an article** called 'The Country The Tourists Never See' for its in-flight magazine. In it you should describe some of the less well-known attractions of your area, and suggest some trips or visits that most tourists would not think of for themselves.

3   You have agreed to lend your flat to an English-speaking friend while you are on holiday. Just before you leave you receive this note.

> I forgot to ask, but how will I get around while I'm staying at your place? I use a bike at home, but would it be safe for me to do the same while I'm at your place? Or should I hire a car or use public transport? I want to make some longer trips as well as going out in your own area. Would you mind leaving me some information and instructions?

Write **detailed notes** to leave in your home, answering all your friend's questions.

4   A group of researchers in the School of Education of an Australian university are advertising in the papers for people from a variety of countries to send them accounts of the education system they experienced. Write your **account**, commenting on what, in your opinion, was good and what was bad in the system you went through.

5   Your local college organizes a competition each year for people who are learning English. This is what they are asking you to do this time.

> Write a review of a film, play or musical show which you have found both entertaining and helpful to you as a learner of English. In up to 250 words, you should give a brief outline of the story, explain why you like it and why you would recommend it as helpful to other English learners.

Write **the review** which you enter for the competition.

PAPER 3   ENGLISH IN USE   (1 HOUR 30 MINUTES)

SECTION A

1   *For questions **1–15**, read the text below and then decide which word on page **17** best fits each space. Put the letter you choose for each question in the correct box on your answer sheet. The exercise begins with an example (**O**).*

GEORGE ORWELL

George Orwell did not expect to be a successful writer. In fact, he (**0**) … much of his life anticipating failure. In an essay about his schooldays, he wrote that until he was about thirty he always planned his life with the (**1**) … that any major undertaking was bound to fail. He wanted success and worked hard to (**2**) … it but he was never quite able to give up the (**3**) … that his efforts would always come up short. At the age of 46, (**4**) … before he died, he confided in his private notebook that a deep (**5**) … of inadequacy had haunted him throughout his career. He stated that there had been (**6**) … not one day in which he did not feel that he was being lazy, that he was (**7**) … with his current job and that his rate of work was miserably small. Even in the first months after the tremendous success of '*Animal Farm*', he was quick to (**8**) … his achievement, declaring that his next book was bound to be a failure.

Of course, no conscientious author is ever completely (**9**) … with their work, but Orwell's doubts were so (**10**) … that he often appeared more comfortable (**11**) … defeat than acknowledging success. In 1940, after the publication of his eighth book, he (**12**) … to an admiring letter from another writer by (**13**) … out of his way to show the man why he was not (**14**) … of his praise. "It makes me laugh," he wrote, "to see you referring to me as 'famous' and 'successful'. I wonder if you (**15**) … how little my books sell!"

0	**A** took	**B** spent	**C** had	**D** followed
1	**A** forecast	**B** trust	**C** expectation	**D** reliance
2	**A** reach	**B** achieve	**C** fulfil	**D** manage
3	**A** impression	**B** notion	**C** judgement	**D** awareness
4	**A** shortly	**B** presently	**C** recently	**D** virtually
5	**A** belief	**B** appreciation	**C** sense	**D** thought
6	**A** totally	**B** fully	**C** constantly	**D** literally
7	**A** behind	**B** below	**C** backward	**D** beneath
8	**A** decrease	**B** discount	**C** refuse	**D** lower
9	**A** cheered	**B** assured	**C** glad	**D** satisfied
10	**A** lengthy	**B** persistent	**C** attached	**D** convinced
11	**A** admitting	**B** granting	**C** agreeing	**D** allowing
12	**A** returned	**B** responded	**C** answered	**D** denied
13	**A** going	**B** moving	**C** setting	**D** leaving
14	**A** capable	**B** worthy	**C** just	**D** acceptable
15	**A** appreciate	**B** assume	**C** regard	**D** acknowledge

Do not forget to put your answers on the answer sheet.

Example:

17

2   *For questions **16–30**, complete the following article by writing each missing word on the answer sheet.* **Use only one word for each space.** *The exercise begins with an example* **0.**

HARRY HOUDINI

Harry Houdini, who died 65 years ago, was the entertainment phenomenon of his era. He (**0**) … escape from chains, locks, ropes and sacks. They strapped him in and hung him upside (**16**) … from a high building and he somehow freed (**17**) … . They locked him in a packing case and sank him in Liverpool docks and minutes (**18**) … he surfaced smiling.

Houdini would usually (**19**) … his equipment to be examined by the audience. The chains, locks and packing cases all seemed fine, (**20**) … it was tempting to conclude that he possessed superhuman powers. However, there was (**21**) … physically remarkable about Houdini (**22**) … for his bravery, dexterity and fitness. His nerve was so cool that he could relax when buried six feet underground (**23**) … they came to dig him up. His fingers were so strong that he (**24**) … undo a strap or manipulate keys through the canvas of a mail bag. He made (**25**) … comprehensive study of locks and was able to conceal tools about his person in a way (**26**) … fooled even the doctors who examined him.

As an entertainer, he combined (**27**) … this strength and ingenuity with a lot of trickery. His stage escapes took place behind a curtain with an orchestra playing to disguise (**28**) … banging and sawing. All Houdini's feats can easily be explained but he (**29**) … to that band of mythical supermen who, we (**30**) … to believe, were capable of miracles.

Do not forget to put your answers on the answer sheet.

Example: | 0 | **could** |

SECTION B

3 In **most** lines in the following text, there is **one** word which is **either** grammatically incorrect **or** does not fit in with the sense of the text. For each numbered line **31–44**, find this word and then write it in the space on your answer sheet. Some lines are correct. Indicate these lines with a tick (✓). The exercise begins with two examples (**0**).

THE ENGLISH LANGUAGE

0	English has for more than a century and a half been called a
0	world language. The number of people who speak it as for their
31	mother tongue has been estimated being at between three
32	hundred million and four hundred million. It is recognised as an
33	official language in countries in where 1.5 billion people live.
34	In China, the importance which attached to learning English is
35	such so that a televised teaching course drew audiences of up
36	to 100 million. But this spread of English throughout the world
37	is being relatively recent. In the late sixteenth century English
38	was spoken by just under five million of people. The arrival of
39	English in North America was the key step in its world-wide
40	expansion. The United States is a huge commercial market and
41	this one has tended to promote the English language in many
42	of other nations. About eighty per cent of the data stored on
43	the world's computers is believed as to be in English and
44	nowadays the insufficient knowledge of English can be a problem
	in business.

Do not forget to put your answers on the answer sheet.

Examples:

0	✓
0	for

4   For questions **45–57**, read the following informal note you have received from a friend and use the information to complete the numbered gaps in the formal notice. Then write the new words in the correct spaces on your answer sheet. **Use no more than two words for each gap**. The exercise begins with an example (**0**). The words you need **do not occur** in the informal note.

INFORMAL NOTE

Jack,

I've got that information you asked me to get about the Young Person's Railcard. It seems that you can only buy one up to March 17th. It looks like a pretty good deal to me because it only costs £35 and you get a lot for that. It allows you to travel anywhere you want for six months and it also lets you pay less at some hotels and restaurants.

You can only get it at the Student Travel Office in Piccadilly and you have to go and get it yourself. It's for people under 26 and you have to prove your age and that you're doing a full-time course. You apply at the office and you have to give them a passport-sized photograph.

It's really a good offer and I think you should encourage any of the students who can do so to get one before it's too late.

Glenn

FORMAL NOTICE

NOTICE TO STUDENTS

THE YOUNG PERSON'S RAILCARD

The Young Person's Railcard is only (**0**) … until 17th March and we advise you to get one because it is very good (**45**) … money. It permits you (**46**) … for six months and it also (**47**) … you to price (**48**) … at certain hotels and restaurants.

It can only be (**49**) … from the Student Travel Office in Piccadilly and it must be (**50**) … . The (**51**) … is 26 and you will need to take (**52**) … your age. You will also need to prove that you are in full-time (**53**) … . At the office, you fill in an (**54**) … and provide a passport-sized photograph.

The card is highly (**55**) … , so if you are (**56**) … for one, remember that you do not (**57**) … in which to buy it.

Do not forget to put your answers on the answer sheet.

Example: | 0 | available

SECTION C

5 *For questions **58–63**, read through the following text and then choose from list **A–K** the best phrase to fill each of the blanks. Write one letter (**A–K**) in the correct box on your answer sheet. **Some of the suggested answers do not fit at all**. One answer has been given as an example (**0**).*

ARUBA

Aruba? Where is Aruba, you may ask. It is a Caribbean island, seventeen miles off the coast of Venezuela. It used to be part of the Dutch West Indies (**0**) .... Aruba is an ancient Indian tribal word meaning buried gold (**58**) .... But the mines are now closed, as are the chemical works and the oil refinery and tourism offers the best hope of economic recovery.

Aruba is an island where all that is beautiful is being preserved in the hope of attracting visitors. And it certainly is beautiful – white beaches, nodding coconut palms, a turquoise sea, reefs of coral and splendid rocks – (**59**) .... It is a genuinely happy island. In a week we did not hear an argument or see a display of bad temper (**60**) .... The number plates on all the cars say it all – *One Happy Island.*

"There is no one day in the year without sunshine," boasts the Aruban Tourist Authority (**61**) .... But the main reason for the friendliness of Arubans is their mixed racial and social background and the fact that, for 350 years, they have never really felt under political pressure. Arubans are easy going, but not lazy. They believe in providing efficient service, but are not servile. They respect tradition (**62**) .... And above all, they believe in keeping their island spotlessly clean.

Aruba is trying hard to provide everything a visitor might want – watersports, good walks and drives, a mass of land sports, casinos and more than 100 restaurants, offering French, Dutch, Italian or Aruban cuisine. But the island's greatest attraction is the good humour of its people (**63**) ....

A and it is true that less than 20 inches of rain fall in a whole year

B but it is not a cheap place to visit

C and nature has given Aruba many such curiosities

D but their lifestyle makes use of the very latest technology

E and the fact that the visitor is not pressurized

F and you have no problem being understood on this island

G and that, anywhere these days, is rare

H and it was this that provided most of the island's wealth in the past

J but it is much more than a beautiful island

K until it gained semi-independence in 1986

Do not forget to put your answers on the answer sheet.

Example: | 0 | K |

6 *Use the following notes to write about California. Write in* **complete sentences** *on the back of Answer Sheet Two for each numbered set of notes, using connecting words and phrases as appropriate.* **Write only one sentence for each set of notes.** *You may add words and change the form of words given in the notes but do not add any extra information. The first point has been expanded for you as an example.*

CALIFORNIA

0 Position and population: Pacific state, USA; pop. 23.5m (largest, USA)

81 Nickname: Golden State (original reason gold mines, more recently sunshine)

82 Main cities: Sacramento (capital), Los Angeles & San Diego (both south), San Francisco (north)

83 Physical features: incl Mt Whitney (highest, USA excl. Alaska), Death Valley (96m below sea level)

84 History: Colony, Spain 1769–1850; state, USA 1850

85 Gold: Jan 1848 discovered, 'gold rush' 1849–56

86 Products: many, incl. fruit, nuts, wheat (leading agricultural state); films, television programmes

87 Electronics: since 1950s many high-technology firms, based Santa Clara county, (known as 'Silicon Valley')

88 Population: 66% non-Hispanic white, 20% Hispanic, 7.5% black, 7% Asian (incl. many Vietnamese)

The space on page 23 can be used for your rough answers.

Do not forget to put your answers on the back of Answer Sheet Two.

0   *California is a Pacific state of the USA, with a population of 23.5 million, which is the largest in the USA.*

81

82

83

84

85

86

87

88

PAPER 4 LISTENING (APPROX. 45 MINUTES)

You will hear a talk about Sick Building Syndrome, which is ill health that is believed to be caused by buildings. For questions 1–12, complete the sentences.
You will hear the recording twice.

SICK BUILDING SYNDROME

According to the World Health Organization, Sick Building Syndrome mostly affects people in __1_____.

Sufferers often lack __2_____.

It mainly affects people early in the week and when they have been __3_____ the building for a long time.

Sufferers often say nothing because they think it is a __4_____ problem.

The problem is not simply a question of the building being __5_____ or having too few windows and too little __6_____.

Buildings most likely to produce the problem are those which have __7_____ and a lot of __8_____.

Experts believe that these lead to poor __9_____, which is the main cause of the problem.

They believe that better __10_____ and design would improve existing systems and that the use of different __11_____ would also help to solve the problem.

In some buildings, better __12_____ has been shown to reduce the problem.

SECTION B

You will hear part of a local radio programme in which details about sports facilities in the area are given. For questions 13–18, fill in the missing details.

Listen very carefully because you will hear the recording only ONCE.

LOCAL SPORTS CENTRES

CENTRE	SPORTS	COACHING
Springfield	swimming diving football	Saturday and Sunday evenings **13** _____ **14** _____
Postbridge	tennis **16** _____	**15** _____ Wednesday evenings
Avenue	tennis **18** _____	**17** _____ Saturday mornings

SECTION C

*You will hear part of a radio programme in which a psychologist talks about the way people behave in crowds and groups. For questions **19–29**, indicate which views he expresses by writing **YES** or **NO** in the box provided. You will hear the piece twice.*

BEHAVIOUR IN CROWDS

People usually only laugh if others are doing so. | 19 |

People hide their real feelings in a crowd. | 20 |

Being in a crowd encourages us to behave badly. | 21 |

Being in a crowd can make us unhappy. | 22 |

Animals only form groups for a specific purpose. | 23 |

Groups of ants and bees have little in common with groups of humans. | 24 |

Our behaviour in crowds is no indication of our real personalities. | 25 |

People often feel restricted when they are members of a group. | 26 |

People are more careful about their behaviour when they're with friends. | 27 |

We change behaviour in groups in the same way as in crowds. | 28 |

Most people do not realize that their behaviour changes according to who they are with. | 29 |

SECTION D

You will hear extracts of five different people talking about events.
You will hear the series twice.

TASK ONE

*Letters **A–H** list different events. As you listen, put them in the order in which you hear them described by completing the boxes numbered **30–34** with the appropriate letter.*

A   a demonstration

B   a concert

C   a sports event

D   a committee meeting

E   a festival

F   a theatre visit

G   an exhibition

H   a party

30	
31	
32	
33	
34	

TASK TWO

*Letters **A–H** list what the people in the five extracts are doing when they are speaking. As you listen, put them in the order in which you hear them by completing the boxes numbered **35–39** with the appropriate letter.*

A   complaining about something

B   refusing to do something

C   joking about something

D   agreeing about something

E   recommending something

F   interpreting something

G   promising to do something

H   insisting on something

35	
36	
37	
38	
39	

1   Why is it strange that so many people can remember what they were doing when President Kennedy was assassinated?

   A   It is difficult to remember your actions on a day a long time ago.
   B   They weren't affected personally by the assassination.
   C   It was such an important event for the world as a whole.
   D   They probably weren't doing anything unusual that day.

2   What does the writer say about the memory in comparison with the computer?

   A   Neither of them is completely reliable all the time.
   B   The memory is more complicated than the computer.
   C   The computer operates in a more organized way than the memory.
   D   Neither of them is used to its fullest capacity all the time.

3   Events enter the long-term memory if

   A   we think about them repeatedly.
   B   we are determined to remember them.
   C   they are repeated many times.
   D   they happen unexpectedly.

4   What do experiments show about our memories?

   A   Our ability to remember something depends on our feelings when it happens.
   B   We are more likely to remember things we do than things we see.
   C   People are more likely to remember pleasant things than unpleasant ones.
   D   We tend to have better long-term memories than short-term memories.

5   The example of wallpaper is intended to illustrate that

   A   most of us pay little attention to our surroundings.
   B   eidetic memories are only useful for remembering visual things.
   C   most of us cannot remember things with complete accuracy.
   D   having an eidetic memory is a big advantage in life.

6   The writer gives an example of using mnemonics for

   A   remembering what something looks like.
   B   remembering where you have put something.
   C   remembering something that you have done.
   D   remembering that you have to do something.

Remember to put your answers on the separate answer sheet.

SECOND TEXT / QUESTIONS 7–24

*Read the following newspaper article and then answer the questions on page **33**. Indicate your answers **on the separate answer sheet**.*

Get busy for a great break

Brave the white water or curl up with a doll. Dymphna Byrne finds activity holidays from the daring to the deliciously lazy

Nothing is quite as relaxing as stretching yourself. If volcano climbing in New Zealand or exploring the remote Knoydart peninsula is too arduous, study Dutch garden design or take a pottery course. Adventure and special interest holidays are booming – a growth area of the travel market.

As well as the perennially popular walking and pony trekking holidays, there is a worldwide mass of water sports, biking and hiking in remote regions and excursions to such inaccessible places as the Orinoco Delta in Venezuela.

Gentler options include courses on doll making or the works of great novelists. Prices range from £2,971 for 20 days in search of the wildlife of Central America to a practical £144 for a four-day walking holiday in North Wales.

One of the best and most informative guides is *Adventure Holidays*. This guide, which gets fatter every year, has thousands of activity holidays in more than 100 countries at prices ranging from £75 for a weekend of rural studies in England to £1,399 for two weeks' riding in Botswana.

The English Tourist Board lists over 200 centres offering activities – deep-sea diving to sailing, bell-ringing to choral singing – in its latest issue of *Let's Do It*, due out in a couple of weeks.

There is plenty of choice for those who are at their best when exercising the body and for those who prefer exercising the mind. The following alphabetical selection includes suggestions.

ACE Study Tours: The Association for Cultural Exchange has been offering immensely popular worldwide study tours for 35 years: art, acting, ecology, wildlife and more. A five-day course on painting, based in a preserved 16th Century Hall in southern England, costs £220, half board. Other courses explore Namibian wildlife, German Gothic architecture and sculpture (0223 835055).

Acorn Activities: This unique organisation was set up two years ago to co-ordinate more than 100 activities throughout Wales. Tailor-made holidays can include hang-gliding, musical instrument playing, walking, painting, arts and crafts and individual French tuition. The quality of instruction is high, accommodation is in farmhouses or hotels. Bed and breakfast from £20, tuition from £30 a day.

Bespoke Holidays: There will be reflected glory in a trek to Everest base camp if the international team reaches the summit. This team will attempt the longest and most difficult west ridge, on the Nepal side of Everest, in late spring. Bespoke Holidays, official agents for the expedition, will run the only authorised trips to base camp. The 22-day trip, with free time in Katmandu, is suitable for anyone capable of managing a couple of walks of seven or eight hours to the base camp. From £1,475 flying from England; from £850 joining in Katmandu (0732 366130).

The Best of Morocco: Morocco, with Mediterranean and Atlantic coastlines, imperial cities, the Sahara desert and the Atlas Mountains (Africa's highest) is rising up the holiday charts. Chris Lawrence has been taking independent travellers there for 25 years and can arrange Land Rover safaris or camel treks in the Sahara, skiing in Oukaimaden, mule trekking, walking, fishing in the Atlas Mountains or golf on the fine courses of Rabat. Seven-day safari from £539 (0380 828533).

Countrywide Holidays: Walking in Britain or in the national parks of Colorado, Utah or Arizona in the US, taking a course in astrology or studying stone circles are among the options. This non-profit organisation, which has just celebrated its centenary, owns 13 houses in some of Britian's finest walking country. There are good rail discounts in Britain and 'adventure and discovery specials' in Malta and Gozo. A week's walking in Britain's undiscovered Lakeland, £245, half board (061 257055).

Explore: Plenty of adventure around the world from this leading company. New tours to Hungary, the Cook Islands and Bhutan give a total of 130 packages in 60 countries. The ability to adjust is more important than fitness in a 15-day adventure to the jungle rivers and waterfalls of the Orinoco. This holiday, with accommodation a mixture of camping and hotels, includes a four-day river journey in canoes. From £1,290 (0252 344161).

HF Holidays: Started in 1913, this company has blossomed in the past few years and now has two walking brochures: one for Britain, the other for the rest of Europe. A third brochure, *Special Interest Holidays in Britain*, has ideas including a week looking into the traditions of Cornwall. Over the years the company has bought comfortable old houses all over Britain and turned them into holiday centres. The atmosphere is friendly and homely and charges are moderate: from £149 full board for a four-day course on the history of English stained glass to £399 for a week of Gaelic Heritage and Traditions in northern Scotland (081 905388).

Naturetrek: A company that has grown with the increased awareness of the environment. Respected naturalists lead groups of 10 to 15 on serious natural history tours: the national parks of Indonesia and southern India, the whales and wilderness of Newfoundland, the Pindos Mountains of northern Greece and so on. From £690 for nine days' bird-watching in the French Pyrenees (096 733051).

Sportif: Those seriously into sport should enjoy the twice-yearly brochure put out by this growing concern that provides a year-round programme of sport for all. Sportif, particularly strong on tennis and wind-surfing, is run by experienced sporting specialists. Mountain-biking, golf and skiing are available; 'suit yourself' holidays can be arranged. A multi-activity week at the Lobos Bahia Club on the sandy island of Fuertaventura provides tennis, squash, wind-surfing, mountain-biking and much more. Tuition available. From £122 per person, four sharing an apartment (0293 567396).

Youth Hostels Association: Rock climbing has long been a speciality of the YHA. Mountain-biking, cross-country skiing, hang-gliding, creative writing, yoga, drawing and painting courses have been added over the years. YHA properties range from former country houses to modern, purpose-built hotels. Some are comfortable, others basic. There is no age limit but YHA membership, which is not expensive, is a must. Holiday prices are moderate. Two days' mountain-biking in Wales, £69; a two-day 'Creating Poetry' course In Ireland, £65 (0727 553215).

Questions 7–17. *Which company offers the following? Choose your answers from the list of companies **A–J**.*
*Note: When more than one answer is required, these may be given **in any order**.*
Some choices may be required more than once.

travel at reduced prices	**7** …………	**A**	ACE Study Tours
holidays in a place that is becoming popular	**8** …………	**B**	Acorn Activities
expert tour leaders	**9** …………	**C**	Bespoke Holidays
accommodation in converted buildings	**10** …………	**D**	The Best of Morocco
	11 …………	**E**	Countrywide Holidays
drama courses	**12** …………	**F**	Explore
travel by boat	**13** …………	**G**	HF Holidays
accommodation with all meals	**14** …………	**H**	Naturetrek
holidays specially organised for individuals	**15** …………	**I**	Sportif
	16 …………	**J**	Youth Hostels Association
travel by animal	**17** …………		

Questions 18–24. *According to the information given, which place would be most suitable for the following kinds of people? Choose your answers from the list of places **A–J**.*

18	people who are very fit	**A**	northern Scotland
		B	Rabat
19	people who are interested in old ways of life	**C**	the French Pyrenees
20	people who are interested in writing	**D**	the Orinoco
		E	Nepal
21	people who want to do a variety of sports	**F**	Germany
22	people who can get used to unusual circumstances	**G**	Fuerteventura
		H	Malta
23	people who want to see wildlife	**I**	Bhutan
24	people who are interested in buildings	**J**	Ireland

Remember to put your answers on the separate answer sheet.

THIRD TEXT / QUESTIONS 25–32

For questions **25–32**, you must choose which of the paragraphs **A–I** on page **35** match the numbered gaps in the following magazine article. There is one extra paragraph, which does not belong in any of the gaps. Indicate your answers **on the separate answer sheet.**

THE ANIMAL DENTIST

Nero, the handsome seven-year-old African lion, can obviously sense, early though it still is, that this is not going to be just another day.

25

The courtyard outside is bustling with people carrying bottles, syringes, drugs, drips and bandages and in half an hour a mini operating theatre is set up right on Nero's doorstep.

26

Nero's broken canine (one of his four front teeth) was spotted by a keeper a few weeks before. "The nerve in the tooth is now totally dead", explains veterinary dentist Peter Kertesz, who has worked on animals' teeth for 14 years.

27

Peter and his assistant Samantha divide their time between working with humans (Mondays to Thursdays) and treating animals (Fridays). Under the name Zoodent International, Peter, 47, performs more dental work on animals than any other practice in the world.

28

"Working with animals is much more difficult than with humans," he says, as Samantha lays out the rows of dental instruments. "You get feedback from people and can develop a relationship with them. With an animal, I have to make an on-the-spot diagnosis and work very quickly."

29

Peter now moves close to the bars of Nero's cage and expertly directs a tiny, plastic blowpipe dart, containing a high dose of anaesthetic, into the lion's thigh.

30

It takes six men to heave the 180 kilogram animal 2 metres from his cage door to the hay mattress that will serve as an operating table. With his huge head lolling helplessly and his tongue hanging from his mouth, Nero looks sadly undignified. But this is an ideal opportunity for Peter to inspect him for any other dental problems.

31

Peter discovers a tooth that needs filling and he sets about doing that first. "This is the same stuff as we use for human teeth," he says, packing the amalgam into the cavity. "There's just more of it."

32

The dental work now over, Peter removes the tube from the lion's mouth. Without the supply of gas, Nero will start coming round fairly quickly, so the keepers move fast to drag him back to his cage. As Peter packs up, the lion stirs. The great yellow eyes are beginning to lose their drugged look. "Don't be fooled," says Peter. "He might appear sleepy but he could react very quickly now if he wanted to …"

A Nero lets out a loud growl before slumping to the floor of his cage. Peter waits for a few minutes before giving the all-clear to unlock the heavy barred door.

B "I often say I've worked on the A to Z of animals, but I actually haven't done a zebra yet," he says, laughing and strapping on rubber knee pads that will allow him to kneel comfortably on Nero's jaws throughout the operation.

C Once the filling is completed, Peter removes the rotten tooth from Nero's upper jaw. He levers it away from its neighbours and tugs it out, leaving a hole which he then stitches up.

D "It could become infected and result in an abscess. An infected tooth may eventually kill an animal once the bacteria enter the bloodstream. A dental problem may also prevent an animal hunting successfully, so it may not be able to feed itself."

E Samantha checks that everything is in place and that they've got enough room to move among all the pipes and tubes surrounding them. Once everything's ready, she signals to Peter that they are all set for the patient.

F He has spent the night in his cage, as usual, but now, when he should be prowling through the Safari Park, he's still here. He paws irritably at the bars of his cage.

G As he roars his disapproval, the lion reveals the badly chipped front tooth that is the reason for all the fuss. Today, the dentist is visiting the king of the jungle.

H "Most pets are fed a balanced diet with the right nutrients and vitamins, but they are not fed a natural diet," says Peter. "The tinned food we feed them doesn't contain the fibre, which is a self-cleaning agent, that a wild animal would eat. Instead, it leaves a sticky deposit that is bad for the teeth."

I A lion-sized prop is inserted into Nero's mouth to keep his jaws apart, followed by a tube from a gas canister to keep him unconscious during the operation. Peter sets to work immediately, examining the great mouth with the help of an endoscope – a long metal tube with a light at its tip.

Remember to put your answers on the separate answer sheet.

FOURTH TEXT / QUESTIONS 33–42

*Read this newspaper article and answer the questions which follow on page **37**. Indicate your answers **on the separate answer sheet**.*

Dreamland
Jim Horne looks at the things we do while we're asleep.

● **Sleepwalking:** Even in the deepest sleep, our thought processes continue. They may be dull or funny. Occasionally, they get out of hand – or out of bed. Sleepwalking, or somnambulism, is now said not to be the enactment of dreams but the reflections of the confused and sometimes anxious thoughts of deep sleep. Common in children, it seems to run in families, peaking in adolescence, and is usually associated with anxiety. It may be trivial – the loss of a favourite toy or just a frustrating day. Only when sleepwalking occurs almost every night is there likely to be more severe underlying distress requiring specific treatment.

Sleepwalkers are unresponsive to their environment, preoccupied with their own thoughts and have no subsequent recall of their nocturnal activities. It is almost impossible to attract their attention. Left alone, they normally go back to bed.

● **Nightmares:** Although nightmares are usually quickly forgotten, they can be very disturbing, particularly if frequent, and if one dwells on them for several days. Whether or not we should place much reliance on trying to interpret their meaning is a matter for debate, as dream interpretation is usually no more than inspired guesswork – with the interpreter fantasising more than the dreamer.

It is normal in sleep for the brain to paralyse the sleeper in order to prevent the acting out of dreams. But sometimes, when waking up suddenly out of a nightmare, this paralysis can continue and one cannot move or call out. This distressing state can take minutes to lift; all the sufferer can do is breathe, move the eyes and possibly moan. In contrast, and in rare circumstances, dreaming may occur without paralysis and then, if the dream is violent, the all too mobile dreamer may come to harm or harm others.

● **Night-terrors:** Whereas the nightmare is visually vivid and prolonged, night-terrors are quite distinct. They are not just bad dreams but sudden and horrifying sensations, with fleeting images that shock the sleeper into immediate wakefulness. Typically, the individual sits abruptly up in bed, screams and appears to be staring wide-eyed at some imaginary scene.

● **Muscle stiffness:** Painful stiffness in the back and shoulders on awakening, that may last for several hours, can be caused by undue muscle tension in the back during sleep. This is often because sleepers have been ruminating too much over disturbing thoughts that seem to plague their minds during sleep. Although sufferers claim to sleep soundly, there is much restlessness in their sleep.

● **Head-banging:** This is common in sleep and is a forward–backward banging of the head into the pillow or mattress, or, worse, into a more solid object. Bouts can last up to 15 minutes. Variants are head-rolling, a repetitive side to side movement and body-rocking, usually performed on the hands and knees, with a backwards–forwards pushing of the head into the pillow. All usually occur at sleep onset and during light sleep. They are commonly found in infants, many of whom seem to get pleasure from the activities.

● **Restless legs:** This is a physical disorder to which older people are susceptible. Although it seems like a form of walking in bed, it has nothing to do with sleepwalking and has a variety of causes. It takes two main forms, one being a sudden jerking or kicking of one or both legs, not just occasionally (which happens to us all now and again in sleep) but every few minutes. The other form is a peculiar creeping sensation in the upper thigh that necessitates shuffling the legs around. Both disorders can severely delay going to sleep and, when sleep eventually comes, the restless legs continue to disrupt it, leaving the individual perplexingly exhausted the next day.

● **Sleeptalking:** This consists of a muttering of jumbled words or phrases with no content. It occurs in light sleep and seldom has anything to do with dreaming. Sleeptalking is common in adults and almost all children do this if talked to during light sleep. But their confused replies have little relevance to what was originally said. If two or more children share a bedroom and one starts sleeptalking, the curtain can go up on the bizarre theatre of the mind, as others join in. None of the participants listens to the ramblings of the other. Each is in a world of his or her own.

Questions 33–42. *Of which of the sleep experiences mentioned in the article are the following statements true?*
Choose your answers from the list of sleep experiences **A–G**.
Note: When more than one answer is required, these may be given **in any order**.
Some choices may be required more than once.

Very young children may appear to enjoy it.

33 . . . .

People who experience it say that they have slept well.

34 . . . .

The person may be very tired afterwards.

35 . . . .

It can be inherited from parents.

36 . . . .

A previous theory about it is no longer accepted.

37 . . . .

Someone experiencing it may make an unhappy sound.

38 . . . .   39 . . . .

It usually starts as soon as the person goes to sleep.

40 . . . .

It means that you are seriously unhappy if it happens repeatedly.

41 . . . .

The person does not react when spoken to.

42 . . . .

A Sleepwalking

B Nightmares

C Night-terrors

D Muscle stiffness

E Head-banging

F Restless legs

G Sleeptalking

Remember to put your answers on the separate answer sheet.

PAPER 2   WRITING   (2 HOURS)

1   A magazine for teachers of English has organized a competition which anyone who teaches school-children can enter. They are invited to share their ideas for making **all** the children they teach enthusiastic learners of English.

*You have been asked to be one of the judges of the competition. Read all the entries carefully and then follow the **Instructions To Judges** and write your report.*

CALLING ALL ENGLISH TEACHERS!
Write and tell us what **you** do to get **all** the children you teach interested in learning English. We'll publish a selection of the best ideas, and you could win a valuable prize for your school!

All signs round our school are written in two languages – our own and English. We label lots of objects with their English names, too, and all the children choose an English name to use in their lessons. A.G.

'Little and often' is the motto at our school. We try to include a short game, song or poem in English in our daily routine – in addition to the usual lessons. K.K.

My colleagues and I give up some of our holiday every year to take a group of children on an educational tour of Britain. They have to speak English all the time while they are away from home. Of course, we spend a lot of time at school preparing them for the trip. S.F.

We've made contact with an American school, and each of our children has a penfriend to send photos, postcards and letters to. Of course, we all write the letters in class together, and the children are always keen to show each other anything they have received from their penfriends. T.P.

At our school we run an English Club one evening every week. Anyone who is interested can come along and do things like watch videos or take part in quizzes. We plan a varied programme, and we try to make sure the activities are always light-hearted and different from the sorts of things we do in ordinary lessons. A.C.

One of the children in my class has an English mother, and she comes in once a week to lead conversations, acting and singing with the children. She helps some of the teachers to improve their spoken English, too! P.L.

INSTRUCTIONS TO JUDGES
Please read the short-list of ideas you have been sent carefully, and then write a report on all of them – the ideas you don't like as well as the ones you think are good. You may organize your report in any way you like, but remember to give reasons for your opinions, and add any general comments you would like to make. Say which entrant you think has the best ideas – entrants are identified by their initials only.

---

*Now write your **report**, in about 250 words.*

SECTION B

*Choose **ONE** of the following writing tasks. Your answer should follow exactly the instructions given. Write approximately 250 words.*

2 Here is part of a letter you receive from an American friend whose parents are about to take a long holiday overseas.

> *My parents will be passing through your part of the country in mid-October. Can you give them some advice about what clothes they will need, and what the weather will be like? What sorts of things can they expect to be able to buy as souvenirs? By the way, if there's anything you would like from the US, please let them know. They'd be glad to bring anything, as long as it isn't too heavy, of course!*

Write **a detailed letter** to your friend's parents, covering all the points raised.

3 You have been asked by an international magazine to write **an article** entitled 'The Changing Family'. Describe any changes in family life you see taking place in your community, and give your opinion on whether life in the family is getting better or worse.

4 Details of a competition have been announced on 'World English Radio'.

> COULD YOU WRITE A RADIO SCRIPT AND READ IT YOURSELF?
> WORLD ENGLISH RADIO OFFERS YOU THE CHANCE TO DO JUST THAT.
> SIMPLY WRITE AN ACCOUNT OF WHAT HAPPENED THE FIRST TIME YOU WENT
> TRAVELLING WITHOUT YOUR PARENTS (IN YOUR OWN COUNTRY OR ABROAD) AND
> SEND IT TO US. WE'LL CHOOSE THE THREE PIECES WE LIKE BEST – THEY'LL
> PROBABLY BE THE THREE MOST AMUSING AND INTERESTING – AND INVITE THE
> WINNERS ALONG TO THE STUDIO TO RECORD THEM.

Write **the account** which you enter for the competition.

5 An international relief agency is asking for volunteers with good practical skills – for example, in medicine, child-care, building or any branch of technology or education – to take a year off from their work or study to help the people of one of the world's poor or troubled countries. Write **a letter of application** for work as a volunteer, giving full details of the skills you have to offer, the kind of place you would prefer to work in and your reasons for applying to be a volunteer.

PAPER 3   ENGLISH IN USE   (1 HOUR 30 MINUTES)

SECTION A

1   *For questions 1–15, read the text below and then decide which word on page 41 best fits each space. Put the letter you choose for each question in the correct box on your answer sheet. The exercise begins with an example (0).*

THE ALEXANDRA PALACE

The Alexandra Palace in north London was built with private (**0**) … as a "People's Palace". Serviced by its own station, it was opened in 1873 and was extremely well (**1**) … until, two weeks after its opening, it burnt down. It was (**2**) … by a slightly larger building which opened in 1875 and featured, (**3**) … other things, a splendid organ and the Great Hall, which was the size of a football pitch. Despite the extraordinarily wide range of events (**4**) … there – from dog shows to great concerts and banquets, from elephant displays to bicycle matches – it always (**5**) … at a loss and by 1877 much of the park around it had been sold to speculative builders, (**6**) … only about half of the original land.

In 1900, a committee was appointed, whose principal duty was to (**7**) … the Palace and park "for the free use of the people forever". There were, however, (**8**) … to charge for entry so that the substantial costs could be (**9**) … . The Palace continued, with (**10**) … degrees of success, as an entertainment centre. In the 1930s it was probably most (**11**) … for being the home of the world's first high definition television broadcasts.

In 1980 the building was once more devastated by fire and (**12**) … to a ruin. It was then decided to (**13**) … it and to create a (**14**) … exhibition centre with community (**15**) … , such as a restaurant and a health club.

0	**A**	sources	**B**	funds	**C**	expenses	**D**	budgets
1	**A**	inhabited	**B**	attended	**C**	crowded	**D**	visited
2	**A**	installed	**B**	overtaken	**C**	renewed	**D**	replaced
3	**A**	among	**B**	between	**C**	from	**D**	around
4	**A**	performed	**B**	set	**C**	staged	**D**	laid
5	**A**	conducted	**B**	acted	**C**	operated	**D**	maintained
6	**A**	letting	**B**	remaining	**C**	leaving	**D**	upholding
7	**A**	run	**B**	handle	**C**	lead	**D**	overlook
8	**A**	powers	**B**	terms	**C**	allowances	**D**	authorities
9	**A**	fulfilled	**B**	covered	**C**	matched	**D**	made
10	**A**	unsteady	**B**	varying	**C**	altering	**D**	unsettled
11	**A**	distinct	**B**	marked	**C**	considerable	**D**	notable
12	**A**	turned	**B**	converted	**C**	reduced	**D**	wrecked
13	**A**	recover	**B**	revise	**C**	restore	**D**	reform
14	**A**	chief	**B**	worthy	**C**	major	**D**	senior
15	**A**	facilities	**B**	conveniences	**C**	supplies	**D**	appliances

Do not forget to put your answers on the answer sheet.

Example: 0   B

2   *For questions* **16–30***, complete the following text by writing each missing word on the answer sheet.* **Use only one word for each space.** *The exercise begins with an example* **(0)***.*

New Horizons

There is a body of literature making forecasts – most of them believable – about the near future and **(0)** … catalogue of predictions is getting fatter by the day.

These predictions range **(16)** … the listing of new devices to the ways **(17)** … which they will alter the daily habits of the citizen. In general, we shall spend more time at home as it **(18)** … easier to communicate without **(19)** … to meet other people – for example, shopping by television and attending video conferences. It is said that it will be easier than ever **(20)** … to leave the house. In fact, **(21)** … narrowing of horizons is already **(22)** … offer, particularly in the field of leisure.

There are computerised programmes **(23)** … the market **(24)** … can take you to visit a museum. You switch on the computer screen and select a route. You enter the room you have **(25)** … and look at the exhibits. You can stop in front of a picture, enlarge **(26)** … detail you may wish to and ask for information. You can stay as **(27)** … as you like, **(28)** … any time of the day or night, **(29)** … meeting any tourists. You don't need to pay an entrance fee – **(30)** … you have to do is connect the computer in the comfort of your own home.

Do not forget to put your answers on the answer sheet.

Example: | 0 | this |

SECTION B

3   In **most** lines of the following text, there is **one** word which is **either** grammatically incorrect **or** does not fit in with the sense of the text. For each numbered line **31–44**, find this word and then write it in the space on your answer sheet. Some lines are correct. Indicate these lines with a tick (✓). The exercise begins with two examples (**0**).

FRESHWATER FISH

0	Freshwater fish have a similar life cycle to birds. The female fish lays eggs
0	but very few of species show any mother-care to their young. Fish are
31	cold-blooded creatures, so it is left as to the water temperature to give the
32	heat that it encourages the egg to hatch into the 'fry', which is the name
33	given to young fish. Small fish crowd together for protection and to learn
34	all the other behaviour that is necessary for their survival. Only very
35	few them learn to escape the attentions of larger fish or the many other
36	predators who live alongside to water. Fish continue to grow throughout
37	the most of their lives. Unlike animals or birds, there is no easily seen
38	child or adult part to their growing up. Fish from healthy waters, where
39	there is plentiful food, will reach to bigger sizes quicker than their less
40	fortunate fellows, who strive to grow in a polluted stretch of water. The
41	feeding style can be readily seen from the position of the each eyes and mouth
42	on many freshwater fish. Generally, those from fish that feed on the bottom
43	of the river or pond have mouths that curve to downward. Surface feeders
44	have a more longer lower jaw.

Do not forget to put your answers on the answer sheet.

Examples:

0	✓
0	of

4 *For questions **45–59**, read the following informal note about problems with a book club and use the information to complete the numbered gaps in the formal letter. Then write the new words in the correct spaces on your answer sheet. **Use no more than two words** for each gap. The exercise begins with an example (**0**). The words you need **do not occur** in the informal note.*

INFORMAL NOTE

Jill,

I rang up that book club of yours while you were away, as you asked me to do. I told them how fed up you are with them and their total lack of efficiency. They told me that you'll have to send them a letter – they won't deal with any complaint on the phone.

So make sure you tell them that they keep sending you the wrong books and bills and not sending you the books you've ordered. Their answer to your last letter – when they said they were looking into it – came ages ago and I think you should tell them that it's just not good enough that they haven't written to you or phoned you since. By the way, the person I spoke to couldn't find any record of these letters and didn't seem to want to help at all – in fact she was rather rude.

I think you should point out what your agreement with them says – you don't have to pay for books you didn't order. And if I were you, I'd tell them that you're not going to give them any more money until the whole thing is sorted out. That should get them to do something about it!

Tony

FORMAL LETTER

Dear Sir/Madam,

A colleague recently telephoned you on (**0**) . . . to (**45**) . . . of my (**46**) . . . at the very poor level of service I have been receiving from you. He was told that I would have to put my complaint (**47**) . . . , which I am now doing.

On numerous occasions, orders and bills have been (**48**) . . . sent and often you have failed to (**49**) . . . with the books I have ordered. (**50**) . . . to my last letter, you claimed that you were (**51**) . . . the matter but this was some time ago and I find it completely unsatisfactory that you have not (**52**) . . . me since. My colleague tells me that you are now unable (**53**) . . . any of our (**54**) . . . and that the person he spoke to was distinctly (**55**) . . . and rather rude.

I feel that I must draw your attention to the fact that, according to (**56**) . . . of our agreement, I am (**57**) . . . to pay for the books I did not order. I am therefore not prepared to make any (**58**) . . . until this matter has been (**59**) . . . .

Yours sincerely

J. Whitaker (Membership Number: 67543-K)

Do not forget to put your answers on the answer sheet.

Example: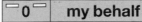

SECTION C

5 *For questions **60–65**, read through the following text and then choose from the list **A–K** the best phrase to fill each of the blanks. Write one letter (**A–K**) in the correct box on your answer sheet. **Some of the suggested answers do not fit at all**. One answer has been given as an example (0).*

Diving Suits

Before the invention of wetsuits in the 1950s, all divers wore 'dry suits', which are still used today for diving in very cold waters. Since the 1800s, divers had been plumbing the depths dressed in waterproof suits topped with huge copper helmets and heavy lead boots. The invention of SCUBA (Self-Contained Underwater Breathing Apparatus) did away with the need for the copper helmets and airlines to the surface and the greater freedom this allowed **(0)** .... .

Although dry suits today **(60)** ... , designed for strength and durability, the basic concept is the same as 50 years ago. The diver is locked into a waterproof case, often with gloves, boots and a hood sealed onto the suit with tight rubber seals. The diver remains dry and insulation **(61)** ... . The diver also wears as much thermal underwear as **(62)** .... .

The first dry suits were latex monstrosities that were difficult to get into and easily torn. During the 1950s and 1960s, dry suits for recreational diving **(63)** ... . In the 1970s the first practical dry suits appeared and the early 1980s saw the introduction of ultra-light dry suits made from nylon. Their added insulation and the comfort factor that the diver stays dry **(64)** ... that would restrict the time underwater for wetsuit wearers. They are less flexible, and certainly less fashionable than wetsuits, and they **(65)** ... for all but the serious diver.

A	can be prohibitively expensive	**G**	make dry suits suitable for extreme conditions
B	can be fitted underneath the dry suit	**H**	were replaced almost exclusively by wet suits
C	can be bought in most good sports shops	**J**	give it remarkable powers of insulation
D	use highly advanced combinations of materials	**K**	paved the way for a more lightweight and flexible generation of dry suits
E	meant wetsuits could be coloured for the first time		
F	is provided by the air trapped in the suit		

Do not forget to put your answers on the answer sheet.

Example:

45

6 *Use the following notes from a leaflet about a college to prepare a letter describing a course. Write in* **complete sentences** *on the back of Answer Sheet Two for each numbered set of notes, using connecting words and phrases as appropriate.* **Write only one sentence for each set of notes.** *You may add words and change the form of the words given in the notes but do not add any extra information. The first point has been expanded for you as an example.*

Computer Training

0	Offered:	intensive courses (5 days); part-time courses (start daily)
81	Location:	Atlanta House – new block, all modern facilities, city centre, convenient buses/trains
82	Hours:	flexible, suit trainees (college open days/eves/Sats)
83	College aim:	trainees learn quickly, improve skills, pleasant surroundings, friendly environment
84	Courses suitable:	absolute beginners / experienced with latest systems / seeking new career opportunities
85	Classes:	max 10; individual tuition guaranteed; trainees progress at own pace
86	Instructors:	all qualified; guidance and encouragement, every stage
87	Fees:	full, in advance (25% discount); instalments (3 x monthly)
88	College Diploma:	approved, most professional bodies; guaranteed or fees refunded

---

The space on page 47 can be used for your rough answers.

Do not forget to put your answers on the back of Answer Sheet Two.

Dear
Thank you for your enquiry, requesting details of our Computer training courses.

0   We offer both five-day intensive courses and part-time courses, which start daily.

81

82

83

84

85

86

87

88

Sandra Pritchard (Admissions Officer)
If you have any further enquiries, please do not hesitate to contact me.

PAPER 4 LISTENING (APPROX 45 MINUTES)

SECTION A

You will hear part of a radio programme, in which the presenter is talking about the attractions of the area. For questions 1–12, make a note of the attractions and what is offered at them.
You will hear the recording twice.

LOCAL ATTRACTIONS

PLACE	ATTRACTION	WHAT'S OFFERED
Halford	1	*reductions for groups*
Linbury	2	*guided tours*
Lewiston	3	*guided tours*
Rockfield	4	5
Buckton	*zoo*	6
Westhill	7	8
Slone	*castle*	9
Loxton	*zoo, especially* 10	*reductions for groups*
Coundon	11	*guided tours*
Trace	12	*children half-price*

SECTION B

You will hear a theatre's recorded information service. For questions 13–21, make a note of the information given.

Listen very carefully because you will hear the recording only ONCE.

YORK THEATRE

"THE DREAM"

Type of play: 13 _____

Tickets: in person from box office

                                       by 14 _____ : phone 071-379-4454

                                       booking fee: 15 _____

Group bookings: reductions for 16 _____ people

Performance time, Sunday: 17 _____

Cheapest tickets: 18 _____ : £5.00

Standby tickets: available 19 _____ before performance

                                       to students, senior citizens and the

                                       20 _____

Applicants must: 21 _____

SECTION C

You will hear a radio programme in which a translator is being interviewed about her job. For questions 22–27, indicate the most appropriate response, A, B, C or D.
You will hear the piece twice.

22 What is the worst problem for translators, according to Fiona?

   A   Some nationalities dislike each other.
   B   It is very difficult to translate jokes.
   C   Some people have no sense of humour.
   D   Personality differences can interfere.

23 Why did she become a translator?

   A   She became interested in the job when she was at university.
   B   Her parents encouraged her to qualify as one.
   C   Learning languages came naturally to her.
   D   Languages were all that she was good at when she was young.

24 What has she found out while being a translator?

   A   It is not possible to understand other cultures fully.
   B   There is too much travelling in the job.
   C   Translators' salaries are far lower than she had expected.
   D   Some people will never get on well together.

25 What did she do in the business meeting?

   A   She defended the other man against her client.
   B   She persuaded the other man to return to the room.
   C   She translated her client's words incorrectly.
   D   She made her client sound more friendly than he was.

26 What happened in the politicians' meeting?

   A   She refused to continue translating.
   B   She did what her client told her to do.
   C   She joined in with the argument.
   D   She left the room during the meeting.

27 What is Fiona's general opinion of her job?

   A   It is no better than many other jobs.
   B   It is better with some languages than with others.
   C   The work is always interesting.
   D   Free time for sightseeing is the best aspect of it.

SECTION D

You will hear extracts of five different people talking about a town.
You will hear the series twice.

TASK ONE

*Letters **A–H** list different people. As you listen, put them in the order in which you hear them by completing the boxes numbered **28–32** with the appropriate letter.*

A a shopkeeper

B a tourist

C a bus driver

D a teacher

E a politician

F a policeman

G a student

H a guide

28	
29	
30	
31	
32	

TASK TWO

*Letters **A–H** list the different topics mentioned by the people speaking in the five extracts. As you listen, put them in the order in which you hear them by completing the boxes numbered **33–37** with the appropriate letter.*

A the amount of public transport

B the range of sports facilities

C the number of tourists

D the amount of entertainment

E the number of jobs available

F the increase in traffic

G the range of shops

H the increase in shoppers

33	
34	
35	
36	
37	

PAPER 5   SPEAKING   (15 MINUTES – 2 OR 3 CANDIDATES)

PHASE A (about 3 minutes)

If you do not know the other candidate, you will be asked to find out about him/her.

Practise asking and answering:

> Where do you come from?
> Tell me something about X. Is it a good place to live?
> What are your special hobbies or interests?
> What do you do?
> Why are you learning English?
> How long have you been learning English?

PHASE B (3 or 4 minutes)

1 Family Group (compare and contrast)

Candidate A should look at picture 2A on page 132
Candidate B should look at picture 2B on page 135

Your pictures are similar but not the same.

Candidate A should describe his/her picture in detail to Candidate B. You have about a minute to do this.

Candidate B should listen carefully. You should then talk about two things which are the same and two things which are different in your picture.

After doing this you can compare your pictures.

2 Market Scenes (describe and identify)

Candidate B should look at the pictures on page 137
Candidate A should look at the pictures on page 134

You each have four pictures. Three of them are the same, but arranged in a different order. One of them is different.

Candidate B should describe all four pictures. You have about a minute to do this.

Candidate A should listen carefully. You should then decide which of your pictures is different from one of Candidate B's. If you need more help, you may ask Candidate B some questions. Say how you decided which picture to choose.

After doing this you can compare both sets of pictures.

PHASE C (3 or 4 minutes)

Images of City Life (discussion)

Both candidates should look at the same set of pictures on page 138. They come from an exhibition of photographs, called 'Images of City Life'. Discuss the impression of city life you get from these particular photos. Is this the aspect of city life you would choose to emphasize if you were taking photographs for this exhibition?

Describe two other photographs you would want to put in this exhibition. Your photos may be similar in theme to the ones shown here, or completely different.

At the end of your discussion you should be able to report your partner's choices as well as your own.

PHASE D (3 or 4 minutes)

What do you consider to be the most and the least attractive features of life in a modern city? Do you think there has ever been a time in the past when city life was more pleasant than it is today? If so, when was that?

What changes do you think will take place in city life over the next ten or twenty years? Talk about, for example, size of population, public and private transport, policing and employment.

How do you feel about the architecture of the modern city? Do you enjoy it, or do you feel that new office buildings are destroying some fine old cities? Do you know a city which is changing rapidly at the moment? Is it changing for the better or worse?

What are the particular stresses and dangers of city life? Would you really avoid these by living in the country?

Can you think of any books or films you know, in which the city setting plays an important part?

TEST 3

PAPER 1 READING (1 HOUR + 15 MINUTES)

FIRST TEXT / QUESTIONS 1–18

Answer questions **1–18** by referring to the magazine article about the early history of the AA (the Automobile Association), printed on pages **54–55**. Indicate your answers **on the separate answer sheet**.

For questions **1–5**, choose the most suitable heading for each of the following sections in the article from the list **A–H** below.

1	Section 1	A	The First AA Garages
2	Section 2	B	Warning Banned
3	Section 3	C	First Road Signs
4	Section 6	D	Roadside Repairs Arrive
5	Section 7	E	The AA Badge Is Born
		F	The First Maps
		G	Other Organisations
		H	Motoring Abroad

Questions 6–18. In which year did the following happen? Choose your answers from the list of years **A–J**.
Note: Some choices may be required more than once.

6	AA patrols in motor vehicles started.		
7	A way of identifying staff was first introduced.		
8	The AA started to operate throughout England.	A	1905
9	Repair establishments were given classifications.	B	1906
10	The AA started to print its own maps.	C	1907
11	The AA published its aims.	D	1908
12	The AA and another organisation joined together.	E	1909
13	A different warning for motorists was introduced.	F	1910
14	Staff were given protection from the weather.	G	1912
15	The AA increased its operating times.	H	1918
16	Lawyers to represent members were introduced.	I	1919
17	Members were first charged for membership.	J	1920
18	A symbol of membership was introduced.		

Remember to put your answers on the separate answer sheet.

THE EARLY YEARS OF THE AA

In the early 1900s the clip-clop of horses' hooves was rapidly being overtaken by the chug-chug of motor car engines. Early motoring, however, was fraught with problems, from pot-holed roads and continual breakdowns to a police force who did little to help, other than arrest drivers for breaking the speed limit. A group of men decided to set up an organisation to help the beleaguered motorists and soon became their champion.

The Automobile Association was formed in 1905. Its aim at the outset was to protect the interests of motorists, by ''patrolling the London to Brighton road and other main roads, as soon as subscriptions were obtained'', with the object of warning motorists of speed traps ahead. A number of keen bicycle riders were paid for by the AA members' subscription fees to check where the police lay in wait and to warn motorists before they reached the spot. Wearing yellow armbands with the AA logo, they would wave at passing motorists if a speed trap lay ahead. And to identify members from non-members, a car badge was produced.

By 1906 the number of permanent patrols approached 40 during the week and nearly 100 at weekends, while membership had reached 3,000.

1	

''Initiate'' was the keyword of the Association in the early years, and this it did. It was responsible for the introduction of the first village name signs. Within ten days of agreeing the idea, up went the first sign, giving the name of the village, the distance from London and the name and distance of the next village along the road, all topped off with the AA badge.

This was followed by the introduction of free legal defence to any member in any proceedings in court under the Motor Car Act. A nationwide chain of solicitors, who were paid a small flat fee for looking after members' interests, was set up.

It was in 1907 that the AA took the first step to change from a Metropolitan organisation into a national one, by opening offices in Manchester and Glasgow.

2	

By 1908 the time had come to look overseas and, with the cooperation of the Touring Club de France, the AA set up its very own Touring Department. This immediately proved itself capable of obtaining all the complicated but necessary papers to take a car into a foreign country, booking ferry tickets, providing local currency, petrol, maps, locations of suitable repair garages and details of hotels.

Shortly afterwards, the AA Committee approved the issuing of the first Handbook. The preface for the 1908 edition spelt out the AA's objectives and all the facilities and services available for members' benefit.

3	

In 1909 an AA patrol was taken to court for signalling to a member who was already in a speed trap, which led to an historic legal judgement.

The basic speed trap consisted of a policeman hidden beside a stretch of road, at the start of a measured distance. When he saw a car travelling too fast, he signalled to another policeman hidden at the end of the measured length of road. The second policeman set a stop watch going when he was signalled to and stopped it when the car passed him. If the car was travelling at more than 20mph, a third policeman further down the road stopped the car and charged the driver with exceeding the speed limit.

In the case of this particular patrol, he had passed the first policeman and, wearing his red AA disc, signalled to a member when he was actually inside the trap and being timed. The defence lawyer stated that the patrol was doing the same duty as the police – checking excessive speed – but the judge took the view that the patrol had not been there to prevent motorists breaking the law but to enable them to evade the consequences.

4   Introducing the Salute

It was a serious blow for the organisation. All AA patrols risked being convicted of obstruction from now on. After losing the case, the Committee decided to change the way that the patrols warned motorists – asking members to stop and talk to any patrol who did not salute them. This was so that he could then tell them of a speed trap on the road ahead.

Next came the uniform. A smart khaki tunic with breeches and leggings and a cap complete with a badge was issued to all patrols. Shortly after, they were given yellow oilskins and "sentry boxes" were erected to enable them to shelter from the cold and the rain. The sentry boxes were soon fitted with telephones, for patrols to assist members who wished to make a call.

In 1910, the AA merged with one of its main competitors, the Motor Union. The joint organisation had a total of 28,040 members. Under the agreement the AA changed its name to the Automobile Association and Motor Union.

5   Hotels Awarded Stars

By 1912 the AA had long been appointing roadside hotels and inns, who were then able to display the AA symbol outside. But motorists wanted to know what kind of accommodation they could expect to find, without going inside the establishment to have a look. Stenson Cooke, the first Secretary of the AA, was familiar with the way brandy was graded by stars and knew that the middling three-star brandy pleased the majority. It was this that sparked off the idea of grading hotels in the same way.

With the outbreak of the First World War, the AA patrols and administrative staff were drastically depleted but the Association continued to support its members with a number of voluntary schemes. During the war, membership dropped from 90,000 until, by 1918 there were only 36,663 AA members. Yet the war had popularised mechanical transport to such an extent that a good number of soldiers proceeded to buy motor-cycles or cars when the war ended and AA membership started to boom again.

That year garages were given stars, much like the hotels; one and two stars were awarded to those with modest motoring supplies; three and four stars for garages equipped to undertake repairs and carrying a range of parts.

6

In 1919 it was decided that patrols on bicycles were not good enough; a fleet of Road Service Outfits – consisting of motorcycles and sidecars – each patrolling 30 miles of roads, was to be introduced as well. The idea was that these would be miniature repair shops, capable of carrying out running repairs to members' cars. And so started the first "breakdown service" provided by the AA.

7

Up to 1920, petrol could only be obtained in two-gallon tins – filling stations, as we know them, did not exist. After a trip to California, the AA's Honorary Treasurer explained that, in America, he could get all the petrol he needed from roadside fuel pumps. The AA, therefore, became the first organisation to set up roadside filling stations in England. Ten were established, spread throughout the country, manned by AA patrols who would serve only members.

Also in 1920, a night service was established at Fanum House in London, providing 24-hour assistance to members. It was a success from the outset.

Maps had been written out by hand in the early days, when a member requested help in getting from A to B. It was agreed to make them widely available by mass production – printing. Later, a group of men from the Routes Department was given a fleet of cars in which to carry out the job of logging every mile an AA member might be likely to travel. More than 30,000 miles were covered in the first season's work.

Then, in February 1920, the long-coveted membership figure of 100,000 was reached.

*Read the following magazine article and then answer the questions on page 57. Indicate your answers **on the separate answer sheet**.*

ACTIONS SPEAK LOUDER THAN WORDS

If you've ever thought that talking to someone was a waste of breath, you might be comforted to know that in some cases you are right – the words we utter have very little effect on people compared with how we say them and what we are doing when we say them.

Recent research has shown that in a presentation before a group of people, 55 per cent of the effect on the audience is determined by the body language of the speaker, 38 per cent by their tone of voice and only 7 per cent by the actual content of what is being said. Body language speaks louder than words. Just try watching a politician on television – what they do is likely to be truer than what they are actually saying.

So can performance and communication skills really be improved? It would appear so, according to something called Neuro-Linguistic Programming, or NLP, which originated in the U.S. It was developed in the 1970s by therapist Richard Bandler and linguistics professor John Grinder. They asked: "What makes the difference between someone who is competent at something and someone who is excellent?" They examined the behaviour of people generally considered to be examples of excellence in their respective fields to identify what they were doing consciously and unconsciously. Surprisingly, they discovered patterns of communication which all these high achievers were using to produce consistently positive results. They found that they were able to copy these strategies and achieve similar success, so they developed a way of teaching these skills to other people, a method they called Neuro-Linguistic Programming.

They have discovered how people achieve mutual understanding, both consciously and unconsciously, by observing the body language and voice patterns of the person they are talking to. If you're dealing with someone who is painfully shy, you're not going to make a good connection by overwhelming them with your cheerfulness. By matching someone's behaviour we can gain their confidence, achieve a good relationship and improve the quality of communication – in other words, we can get on someone's wavelength.

NLP practitioners claim anyone can learn how to do this, and quite quickly. You don't have to be 'good with people'. You can observe certain signals conveyed in posture, gesture and eye movements, all of which reveal how people are really feeling – a reality which may belie the words they are using. We have all had the experience of asking somebody "How are you?" and hearing "Oh, fine …", a reply that is loaded with the suggestion that the speaker is depressed. The unconscious process that leads us to that conclusion is what NLP is all about – taking an unconscious, not very highly developed skill and practising it consciously.

Another powerful aspect of NLP is its use of suggestion and positive thinking. We can become aware of the negative and turn it to the positive. Once it is framed in a positive way as a goal, the brain can begin to grapple with it and then apply itself to achieving that outcome. To put it another way, if you don't know where you're going, it makes it harder to get there. "I wish I weren't so shy" is no good as a goal. "I want to be confident, relaxed and outgoing when I meet new people" tells you exactly what you want and gives you some clues as to how you could modify your behaviour to achieve it.

At some level we already know this. What's the best way to make someone, particularly a child, drop something? Say "Mind you don't drop it." If you tell children "Don't make a mess", a mess is undoubtedly what they will make. You have announced your expectations. You've already visualised the tray being dropped, the room being untidy and, surprise, the wheels are set in motion and what we warn against is what happens.

So, avoid making negative statements. Instead, try saying "Could you please keep the room tidy?" or "Make sure you keep those drinks on the tray." Immediately, you have a more positive image of the desired outcome of events and your brain and body become subconsciously programmed to achieve it.

NLP can be applied to any area of human activity. It has been used to cultivate excellence in sport, training, business, education, music and the arts. Managers find their managerial skills improved, salespeople learn how to adapt their presentation to the customer, and educators find ways to involve students more fully.

19   What has recent research into the way people speak shown?

    A   Certain kinds of body language create distrust.

    B   A person's tone of voice often does not match what they are saying.

    C   Politicians are seldom considered to be telling the truth.

    D   Failure to communicate well has little to do with what you say.

20   The therapist and the professor developed NLP when they discovered that

    A   successful people communicate in similar ways.

    B   people copy methods of communication.

    C   competence depends on good communication.

    D   people in different professions communicate differently.

21   According to NLP, what is the most important ingredient in successful communication?

    A   confidence

    B   clarity

    C   sincerity

    D   sensitivity

22   NLP training involves learning how to

    A   increase an ability that we already have.

    B   improve our ability to communicate feelings.

    C   be more aware of our own body and eye movements.

    D   respond more quickly to what people say to us.

23   Which of the following does NLP teach people to do when communicating with others?

    A   realise when they are making mistakes

    B   behave in the way that the others do

    C   decide precisely what their aims are

    D   stop thinking about what they are doing

24   According to NLP, what would be the best thing to say to somebody who is often late?

    A   Make sure you're not late again.

    B   It'll please me if you're on time.

    C   I'll be angry if you're not on time.

    D   You won't be late again, will you?

Remember to put your answers on the separate answer sheet.

THIRD TEXT / QUESTIONS 25–36

*Answer questions **25–36** by referring to the article giving advice to salespeople, printed on page **59**. Indicate your answers **on the separate answer sheet**.*

*For questions **25–31**, answer by choosing from the sections of the article **A–O**.*

Which section refers to:

25   talking about the disadvantages of other products

26   deciding it is wise to give up on a sale

27   failing to communicate confidence in the product

28   being distrusted by the customer

29   putting a direct question to a customer

30   not being put off by the customer's reaction

31   making the customer feel good

*For questions **32–36**, choose the most suitable headings for the following sections of the article from the list **A–H** below.*

32	Section C	**A**	I made it all too complicated
33	Section D	**B**	I gave the wrong information
34	Section E	**C**	I didn't look right
35	Section G	**D**	I didn't plan ahead
36	Section J	**E**	I spent too long with the customer
		F	I couldn't give the details
		G	I should have let the customer speak
		H	I didn't make it sound attractive

Remember to put your answers on the separate answer sheet.

15 Ways To Lose a Sale

Self analysis and criticism are the only real ways we can improve our individual performance and abilities. This is especially true for salespeople.
The reasons why a potential customer buys or doesn't buy are countless. Here are just 15 ways to lose a sale ...

The potential customer didn't buy because:

A	I exaggerated

The recipe of the con-artist. Once your potential customer has decided that you've exaggerated on one part of your presentation, the rest of what you have to say is also suspect.

B	I misrepresented

One step up from exaggeration. Stick to the facts, persuade with information – supportable information.

C	

Make sure you have something to sell your potential customer before you take up his or her time. They could be half way to a "No" as soon as they see that you don't know what to do next.

D	

You won't learn a thing while YOU are talking. Slow down, say what you have to say and give the potential customer a chance to voice their opinions or objections. They may be waiting for the chance to say YES.

E	

This means turning the facts, figures and terminology into charts, graphs and word pictures the potential customer can follow. It is possible to sell an idea then make it all so complex that the potential buyer never gets around to buying. If you confuse the issues rather than clarify them, you'll make it difficult for the potential buyer to say YES.

F	I was awkward

Familiarise yourself with the tools you intend to use. Practise your presentation and keep practising to overcome any awkwardness.

G	

Know your products! You must inform in order to persuade. If you cannot answer questions on the spot, make sure you find the answer as soon as possible and get back to the client.

H	I went straight to the boss

Strive for a top management decision but sell all the way up. Sell to the receptionist, clerks, buyers, personal assistants or whoever! Sell them yourself and your organisation and they will help you close the sale with management.

I	I used high pressure

This is the desperate bid of the 'once-only' salesperson. It is better to use your intelligence and lose a sale than to use high pressure and lose the client altogether.

J	

People like to deal with successful people and rightly or wrongly, your immediate success is judged by your appearance. Make sure it counts for you and not against you.

K	I knocked my competition

Don't waste your time trying to destroy the competition. Concentrate on selling positively the value and results of your own product or service. Emphasise the difference only if the client wants comparisons.

L	I let the buyer scare me

Tough buyers thrive on defeating ill-equipped salespeople. They tend to give in when they meet a salesperson who overcomes objections in a confident, friendly manner and turns the conversation back on course.

M	I showed no enthusiasm

Enthusiasm is catching – spread it around. Start with a bigger than normal smile. Few potential clients want to spend money. You must give them confidence in their buying decisions and nothing helps like enthusiasm.

N	I didn't make it a good buy

Buyers often resent salespeople whose approach is too humble. You must convey to the potential customer the value and potential of the service or product they are buying. Describe the benefits of the results.

O	I didn't ask the customer to buy

The least you can do is give the client the opportunity to say YES, NO or MAYBE. Make it easy for them – ask them!

FOURTH TEXT / QUESTIONS 37–44

For questions 37–44, you must choose which of the paragraphs A–I on page 61 match the numbered gaps in the following newspaper article. There is one extra paragraph, which does not belong in any of the gaps. Indicate your answers on the separate answer sheet.

Beethoven's Piano

In 1817 the English piano maker Thomas Broadwood met Beethoven in Vienna and promised him the gift of a piano.

37

Beethoven kept it until his death in 1827, reputedly using it to write, among other things, the *Hammerklavier* sonata. Then it passed to Liszt, who left it to the Hungarian National Museum in Budapest.

38

This time, though, the piano is working its passage, on a concert tour sponsored by Broadwood's (the firm still exists).

39

Why is this piano so important? Well, it *is* an icon. It featured prominently in Beethoven's later years and the very abuse to which he subjected it, hammering at the notes to try to hear them, records the terrible pathos of Beethoven's deafness.

40

But bringing this Broadwood back to life is also a landmark in the modern history of performance, recognising that old instruments offer unique insights into old music – and none more than pianos in the time of Beethoven when their technology was young and fast-developing, and composers responded immediately to the latest thing on the market.

The novelty of the Broadwood was a heavier action which meant that, whatever his hearing impairment, Beethoven could feel he was making more sound than a Viennese piano could deliver. It was harder work but it gave a better sense of control and a more consistent, more modern sound across its range.

41

For a player like Melvyn Tan, those limitations are critical because they demonstrate how Beethoven's writing pushed the piano to its physical extremities. It's important not to lose the limitations when a piano is restored.

42

David Winston, the restorer admits: "It's true that every time you restore you lose original information. So I have to ask myself: will this work increase the piano's lifespan, and is it reversible? And I document everything so it's clear to someone 50 years from now exactly what I've done."

43

Winston's work has left the Viennese input alone but removed the rest. He has replaced the strings, which weren't original, the dampers and the hammer coverings. Otherwise, he says, the piano was in decent structural condition. "It was chosen in the first place to be robust, and it is." However, the present tour has raised a musicological question for Tan.

44

So either he didn't write *Hammerklavier* on the Broadwood after all or he wrote it idealistically, beyond the character and limitations of the instrument at hand.

A   The Broadwood had in fact been regularly tampered with – from when it first arrived in Vienna to more recent times when it was patched up by Hungarians without access to the right materials.

B   He could afford it – Broadwood's was the most successful piano company in the world   and a model was dispatched from London on 27 December, by sea through the Straits of Gibraltar to Trieste and then by cart to Vienna, arriving the following June.

C   By 1824 a friend observed that "there was no sound left in the treble and broken strings were mixed up like thorns in a gale."

D   The ethics of restoration are contentious. Not everyone agreed that Beethoven's Broadwood should be returned to playing condition, still less taken on tour.

E   He has found it difficult to programme the tour because – and this is slightly embarrassing – few of the scores Beethoven supposedly wrote on the Broadwood are playable on it. The keyboard is too short.

F   There it remained, a national treasure, seen but barely heard, until it began a journey almost as momentous as the one all those years ago, back through Europe to Britain.

G   George Bernard Shaw said that the most entirely creditable incident in English history was the sending of £100 to Beethoven on his death-bed by the London Philharmonic Society. But there was another.

H   Like all great stars (and this one is insured for £5m) it travels with an entourage. There is the pianist Melvyn Tan who plays it, the piano doctor David Winston who restored it, four attendants who transport it between venues by unpublishable routes, and two security men who sleep with it.

I   But, of course, it's *not* a modern sound. It still has the limitations of its time, including a slight twang, a noisy action and ineffectual dampers.

Remember to put your answers on the separate answer sheet.

PAPER 3   ENGLISH IN USE   (1 HOUR 30 MINUTES)

SECTION A

1   *For questions **1–15**, read the text below and then decide which word on page **65** best fits each space. Put the letter you choose for each question in the correct box on your answer sheet. The exercise begins with an example (**0**).*

THE MOTORING BOOM IN THE US

The 1920s saw the emergence of widespread car ownership in the US. Assembly-line (**0**) … made cars wonderfully cheap, credit was available on the cheapest (**1**) … and the irresistible (**2**) … of the car to the consumer did the rest. The result was a complete (**3**) … of American life.

The car began to break (**4**) … the ancient sharp division between town and country. The movement perhaps began with the prosperous middle class, (**5**) … for a holiday from New York, who were delighted to discover the rest of their country. But the cheap car also enabled the working class to travel, for pleasure or in (**6**) … of work. Even poor country people, it (**7**) … out, could own cars and when they did so, many of them used the freedom thus (**8**) … to depart – to the West or to the cities.

Even more important, perhaps, was the (**9**) … of the car on daily life. It came into (**10**) … for all sorts of short (**11**) …, to work or to the shops, which had previously been made by trolley bus or railway. It made a whole new pattern of living possible. Vast suburbs began to (**12**) … over the land. No longer did you have to live in comparatively cramped (**13**) … near the railroad station. Nor did you have to (**14**) … your annual holiday at one of the traditional, crowded resorts nearby. Instead, you could (**15**) … over the hills and far away.

0	**A** process	**B** system	**C** production	**D** creation
1	**A** obligations	**B** terms	**C** guarantees	**D** repayments
2	**A** appeal	**B** outlook	**C** impression	**D** fancy
3	**A** transfer	**B** variation	**C** revision	**D** transformation
4	**A** down	**B** off	**C** in	**D** away
5	**A** concerned	**B** willing	**C** anxious	**D** fond
6	**A** hunt	**B** search	**C** chase	**D** inquiry
7	**A** found	**B** turned	**C** brought	**D** set
8	**A** gained	**B** gathered	**C** reached	**D** benefited
9	**A** force	**B** product	**C** impact	**D** trace
10	**A** advantage	**B** use	**C** worth	**D** function
11	**A** travels	**B** trips	**C** tours	**D** routes
12	**A** spread	**B** widen	**C** scatter	**D** broadcast
13	**A** housing	**B** residence	**C** surrounding	**D** settlement
14	**A** make	**B** place	**C** take	**D** set
15	**A** press	**B** speed	**C** stir	**D** pace

Do not forget to put your answers on the answer sheet.

Example:

65

2 *For questions 16–30, complete the following article by writing each missing word on the answer sheet.* **Use only one word for each space**. *The exercise begins with an example (0).*

GRAPEFRUIT

Grapefruit are members of the citrus family. They are one of the largest citrus fruits, (0) … juicy flesh that has a sharp flavour. The white-fleshed varieties are slightly more acidic in taste than sweeter pink grapefruit, (16) … have few pips and more juice.

The true reason behind the name of (17) … refreshing fruit is not known, (18) … it is thought to be because grapefruit grow in clusters, rather like grapes, (19) … an evergreen tree. However, records from the early 19th century refer to grapefruit (20) … having the taste of sour grapes and bearing their name (21) … this very reason.

Grapefruit are thought to (22) … originated in Jamaica. In England, they were first written (23) … in the *Daily Chronicle* in 1904, when it was reported that "the grapefruit is gradually growing (24) … popularity in England." At this time, writers were never sure (25) … to hyphenate the name or leave it as (26) … word. By 1938, grapefruit were well known and the famous London store Fortnum and Mason advertised special knives to prepare them, (27) … sale at 3 shillings each.

There are several varieties, (28) … with its own special characteristics. Choose firm grapefruit, with bright shiny skin. The fruit should feel heavy in relation (29) … the size (30) … this indicates plenty of juicy flesh.

Do not forget to put your answers on the answer sheet.

Example: | 0 | **with** |

SECTION B

3   In **most** lines of the following text, there is **either** a spelling **or** a punctuation error. For each numbered line **31–43**, write the correctly spelled word(s) or show the correct punctuation in the spaces on your answer sheet. Some lines are correct. Indicate these on your answer sheet with a tick (✓). The exercise begins with three examples (**0**).

Mobile phones

0	The next genneration of telephone users will laugh when we explain
0	how we used to stand next to a wall in the kitchen to make a phone
0	call. Mobile communications already highly advanced compared with
31	a decade ago, will completly alter communications in the next few
32	years. Though there are millions of people using mobile phones most
33	people know little about the mobile telecommunications industry and
34	its tecnology. There are three types of mobile phone. These are hand
35	portables mobiles and transportables. The smallest and most popular
36	are the pocket-sized hand portables. These work on rechargeable
37	batteries, which allow an average of up to 80 minute's conversation.
38	Mobiles are fited permanently in a vehicle, so do not rely on
39	seperate batteries. They require an external aerial on the vehicle.
40	This can mean a stronger signal with clearer speech. Transportables
41	have a hight power capability and can be used almost anywhere.
42	They come with a powerful battery pack for longer, continuos use
43	and may also be put into a vehicle, using it's electrics. They tend
	to be bulkier than hand portables.

Do not forget to put your answers on the answer sheet.

Examples:

0	generation
0	✓
0	communications, already

4   *For questions **44–58**, read the following public announcement about a music competition and use the information to complete the numbered gaps in the informal letter. Then write the new words in the correct spaces on your answer sheet. **Use no more than two words** for each gap. The exercise begins with an example (**0**). The words you need **do not occur** in the public announcement.*

PUBLIC ANNOUNCEMENT

COMPETITION FOR LOCAL MUSICIANS

This is the tenth year of our annual competition, which is open to all local musicians. Whether you play or sing, alone or in a band or orchestra, we'd like you to enter. Classical, rock, or any other kind of music, we'd like to hear you. Our competition takes place from June 12th to June 19th in the Central Hall in front of a large audience and a jury of five. Competitors may perform any piece of their choice, including one they have composed themselves, provided it does not exceed the limit of 15 minutes.

Prizes:
Winners: time in a recording studio without charge and a TV appearance
Runners-up: an instrument of your choice

Interested?: Telephone Paula Sheen on 0989-54634

INFORMAL LETTER

Dear Rick,

Have you heard about the competition for local musicians that they hold (**0**) . . . ?. Well, I've been thinking that maybe we should (**44**) . . . for it. (**45**) . . . enter and it doesn't matter whether you perform on (**46**) . . . or as a group. So I reckon we should (**47**) . . . our own band – it shouldn't be too difficult to find another couple of people to join us.
They hold the competition over a week in June in the Central Hall and apparently quite a big (**48**) . . . turns up for it. Oh, and it says that there are five (**49**) . . . . We can play one of the songs we've (**50**) . . . – we don't have to play something by someone else. It says that you can play anything you like (**51**) . . . as it doesn't (**52**) . . . than fifteen minutes.
The winners get (**53**) . . . of a recording studio and the chance to (**54**) . . . TV. If you (**55**) . . . , you can have any instrument (**56**) . . . .
So, what do you reckon? Shall we have a go? Apparently, anyone who's interested has to get (**57**) . . . with someone called Paula Sheen. (**58**) . . . is on the advert, so if you do fancy it, I can do that. Let me know as soon as you can.

All the best,
Phil

Do not forget to put your answers on the answer sheet.

Example: | 0 | every year

SECTION C

5 *For questions **59–64**, read through the following text and then choose from the list **A–K** the best phrase to fill each of the blanks. Write one letter (**A–K**) in the correct box on your answer sheet. **Some of the suggested answers do not fit at all**. One answer has been given as an example (**0**).*

Hay Fever

Hay fever is the most common allergy there is. It is widespread among children and teenagers, (**0**) .... You are also prone to hay fever if you have another allergy and, like other allergies, it seems to run in families. What's more it's on the increase – studies throughout Europe show a steady growth in the number of sufferers in the past 20 years.

Hay fever has little to do with hay. It's actually caused by pollen from trees, grasses and weeds (**59**) .... When sufferers come into contact with pollen-laden air, their immune system starts working overtime (**60**) ... which trigger all the classic hay fever symptoms – a stuffy, runny nose, sneezing, an itchy or sore throat and watery eyes. Although the hay fever season peaks in June and July, some people are allergic to tree pollens released in February and March (**61**) ....

Weather is all-important. It determines when the hay fever season starts (**62**) .... The cooler and drier the spring, the later the season. Pollen counts are lower on dull, damp days – (**63**) ... – and higher on hot, dry days. Wind dilutes pollen, so sufferers should make for the coast where sea breezes blow the pollen away. Mountain regions are another haven (**64**) .... Cities also have lower pollen counts than country areas. In low-lying grassland regions the count can be five times higher than in cities, although there's now evidence that city pollutants can bring on hay fever symptoms.

A and others react to weed pollens that are around from spring to autumn	**F** which can make the problem worse
	G which is dispersed into the air during spring and summer
B which helps cleanse the air of pollen	
C and splash your eyes with water	**H** and releases histamines and other chemicals
D when less pollen is lifted off the plants	**J** as their climate and altitude keep counts low
E and how much pollen is in the air each day	**K** although they often grow out of it

Do not forget to put your answers on the answer sheet.
Example: **0**   **K**

6 *Use the following notes to write about the Wimbledon Lawn Tennis Championships. Write **in complete sentences** on the back of Answer Sheet Two for each numbered set of notes, using connecting words and phrases as appropriate. You must write **only one sentence** for each set of notes. You may add words and change the form of words given in the notes but do not add any extra information. The first point has been expanded for you as an example.*

THE WIMBLEDON LAWN TENNIS CHAMPIONSHIPS

0 Oldest tennis tournament in world; surface: grass

81 Where: All England Club, Wimbledon (suburb, SW London)

82 When: fortnight – last week June, first week July – every year

83 Started: 1877 (men only), first winner Spencer Gore (British)

84 The Club: 18 courts, biggest Centre Court (finals played there) + No. 1 Court

85 Amateurs only 1877–1968; professionals allowed 1968+

86 Martina Navratilova (9 times women's champion) + Bjorn Borg (5 times men's champion) = winners of championship most times

87 Last British champion: men – Fred Perry (3 times 1934–36); women – Virginia Wade (1977)

88 One of 4 main tournaments (others: Australian, French, US Opens), together = "Grand Slam"

The space on page 71 can be used for your rough answers.

Do not forget to put your answers on the back of Answer Sheet Two.

0   *The Wimbledon Lawn Tennis Championships is the oldest tennis tournament in the world and is played on grass.*

81

82

83

84

85

86

87

88

PAPER 4   LISTENING   (APPROX. 45 MINUTES)

You will hear a talk about the country Malawi. For questions 1–12, complete the sentences.
You will hear the recording twice.

Malawi

Malawi ceased to be a British colony **1** _____ .

It has a very large lake, which is as **2** _____ England.

Because there are **3** _____ , you have to use
4 _____ to get from the ship to the shore.

The ship brings **5** _____ to the villages in the North.

Fish are caught on **6** _____ of the lake.

In the villages by the lake they have no **7** _____ or
8 _____ supply.

They entertain themselves with **9** _____ music and
instruments.

There are about 1,000 **10** _____ in the lake, many of them
discovered **11** _____ .

The lake is not affected by **12** _____ .

SECTION B

*You will hear the presenter of a programme about animals giving details of a scheme. For questions **13–18**, fill in the missing information.*

Listen very carefully because you will hear the recording only ONCE.

Animal Watch	
Scheme operated by:	*a zoo*
	13 [ ]
Aims:	*to raise awareness and* **14** [ ]
Examples of projects:	*to protect rhinos from* **15** [ ]
	to return animals to the wild
Benefits to members:	*free entry to the two institutions for a year*
	three editions of **16** [ ] *magazine*
	17 [ ] *at shops*
Application forms:	*at the two institutions*
	18 [ ]

SECTION C

You will hear a radio interview with a husband and wife who write books for children together. For questions **19–28**, indicate whether the views are expressed in the interview by writing **YES** or **NO** in the box provided.
You will hear the piece twice.

Children's Book Writers

It's easier to write a book with someone else than alone.   **19**

The drawings in children's books should be completely realistic.   **20**

It is better if one person does the research and the other does the final version.   **21**

Children's books should be amusing for parents too.   **22**

Children's books should also have a serious purpose.   **23**

Characters in children's books sometimes frighten them.   **24**

Children's books should contain a large variety of things.   **25**

Children's books should be read from start to finish in one go.   **26**

Some children dislike the whole idea of books.   **27**

Children's books often have unattractive titles.   **28**

SECTION D

You will hear extracts of five different people talking about items they have recently bought.
You will hear the series twice.

TASK ONE

Letters **A–H** list different items. As you listen, put them in the order in which you hear them being talked about by completing the boxes numbered **29–33** with the appropriate letter.

A   a computer

B   a fridge/freezer

C   a vacuum cleaner

D   a washing machine

E   a cooker

F   a hi-fi system

G   a television and video recorder

H   a coffee machine

29	
30	
31	
32	
33	

TASK TWO

Letters **A–H** list the different opinions expressed by the people speaking in the five extracts. As you listen, put them in the order in which you hear them by completing the boxes numbered **34–38** with the appropriate letter.

A   it will last a long time

B   it's too complicated

C   it doesn't work properly

D   it looks nice

E   it's too big

F   it's a waste of money

G   it's very noisy

H   it was a bargain

34	
35	
36	
37	
38	

PAPER 5   SPEAKING   (15 MINUTES – 2 OR 3 CANDIDATES)

PHASE A (about 3 minutes)

If you do not know the other candidate, you will be asked to find out about him/her.

Practise asking and answering:

> Can you tell me something about your family?
> Do you have any brothers or sisters? Tell me something about them.
> Do you live with your parents?
> How are you hoping to use English in the future?
> What sort of job are you hoping to get?

PHASE B (3 or 4 minutes)

1 Soft Sculpture (describe and relate)

Candidate A should look at picture 3A on page 132
Candidate B should look at picture 3B on page 135

Your pictures are similar but not the same.

Candidate A should describe his/her picture in detail. You have about a minute to do this.

Candidate B should listen carefully. You should then talk about two things which are different in your picture, and about how the pictures are related to one another. If you need more help, you may ask Candidate A some questions.

After doing this you can compare your pictures.

2 Balloon Seller (describe and compare)

Candidate B should look at the pictures on page 135
Candidate A should look at the pictures on page 132

You each have two pictures, 3C and 3D. One of them is the same for both of you, but the other is similar, but not the same.

Candidate B should describe both of his/her pictures in detail. You have about a minute to do this.

Candidate A should listen carefully. You should then say which picture is the same, and talk about the most important differences between the other pictures. If you need more help, you may ask Candidate B some questions.

PHASE C (3 or 4 minutes)

Grandad's New Motorbike (evaluation and discussion)

Both candidates should look at picture 3E on page 139 and discuss it. Talk about the age, attitudes and sort of life you think the man leads.

Try to decide what the purpose of this picture is, and suggest a title for it.

If your partner has different ideas from yours, be prepared to describe them.

PHASE D (3 or 4 minutes)

What did you decide about the picture? In fact, it advertises financial planning for older people. The title is 'Grow Old Disgracefully', and the advert begins 'Why slow down as you get older?'

Can you explain the meaning of 'Grow Old Disgracefully'? How does this differ from more traditional attitudes to ageing?

In what ways do you think people **should** change their lifestyles as they get older? Are there any things older people can't or shouldn't do? Can you think of any old people you particularly admire? Think of examples from among people you know, or famous people.

The term 'ageism' is sometimes used to describe social prejudice against older people. Does it exist, in your opinion, and how might it affect people's lives?

Some people hate the thought of retiring from their jobs, while others want to retire as early as possible. What sorts of reasons do you think there are for this? Should there be a fixed age when people have to retire?

TEST 4
PAPER 1   READING   (1 HOUR + 15 MINUTES)

FIRST TEXT / QUESTIONS 1–18

*Read this magazine article and answer the questions which follow on page **79**. Indicate your answers **on the separate answer sheet.***

Doodles

Some of us doodle all the time, others only occasionally. And there are people who say that they never do – though a closer look at the notepad next to their telephone, this week's shopping list or the odd empty envelope may tell a different story. To the trained eye, every little scribble we make betrays our hidden desires, strengths and weaknesses. What do our doodles mean? Expert Gloria Hargreaves reveals what lies behind the lines we draw and the scribbles we make in idle moments.

BIRDS
A large, simply outlined bird shows a clear thinker with a very demanding conscience and definite ideas of right and wrong. A flying bird signifies someone who is tolerant and broad-minded. High-flying gulls are the sign of a relaxed, easy-going person.

BOXES
A line of boxes indicates someone who's unlikely to do anything surprising. Boxes piled neatly on top of one another show a person who's tidy and well-organised. Boxes within boxes shout 'let me out' and suggest that you're feeling trapped.

CIRCLES
Circles within circles indicate someone who can be hard to pin down. They will have an answer to any question, although it may not necessarily be the one you want to hear! They are very adaptable and tend to go with the flow. Overall, they have a very likeable, provocative personality and a positive frame of mind.

FLAGS
A simple, triangular flag indicates a competitive, aggressive nature or someone who is concise and to the point. A square flag shows a steady, practical person with both feet firmly on the ground. A heavily shaded flag indicates nervousness, depression and uncertainty about a decision already taken.

LINES
Scribbling a series of short, straight horizontal lines signifies a reliable person, able to stay calm in a crisis. Lines which go up at the end show someone who is enthusiastic and good fun. A series of vertical lines suggests feelings of frustration and disappointment. Drawn with heavy pressure, they indicate aggression, too. Wiggly lines suggest someone subject to mood swings. Jagged lines show confusion and the inability to make decisions.

MOUNTAINS

By drawing mountains, you reveal a desire to succeed. If they are neatly laid out they indicate a good organiser who doesn't like leaving things to chance and a person who is happiest when in control.

QUESTION MARKS

These can indicate that you like to know other people's business and usually find out what you want to know. A series of question marks suggests that you enjoy solving other people's problems. If you produce a pattern based on a question mark, this means that, although you started with a problem, you have now worked out what the answer is.

STAIRS

To draw rising stairs signifies that you have qualities of leadership and that you love a challenge. You are ambitious in your career, but happy to encourage others, too. If your steps almost fill the page, your goals are founded in fantasy. A series of steps or staircases means that you will try and try again. Not easily put off or discouraged, you would make an excellent salesperson.

STICK FIGURES

The use of stick figures shows a highly intelligent person who is not to be underestimated. If they are drawn with a mixture of rounded and angular movements, they indicate someone with a soft exterior, but who can be tough if they need to be. Such a person usually gets what they want but is always nice about getting it.

TREES

A winter tree shows an impatient person with a critical nature. A Christmas tree signals a rather fussy character who may be sarcastic and aggressive when under pressure. A weeping willow indicates that you're feeling fed up at the moment.

Questions 1–18. *What kind of doodle may indicate the following type of person? Choose your answer from the list ot kinds of doodle **A–J**.*
Note: Some choices may be required more than once.

1	someone with a strong sense of morality		
2	a person whose behaviour is predictable		
3	someone whose feelings are always changing		
4	a person with unrealistic aims		
5	someone who makes enjoyable company	**A**	BIRDS
6	a person who does not let other people down	**B**	BOXES
7	someone who likes to do difficult things	**C**	CIRCLES
8	a person who likes hearing gossip	**D**	FLAGS
9	someone who says things which may offend	**E**	LINES
10	a person who reacts badly to problems	**F**	MOUNTAINS
11	someone who can accept other points of view	**G**	QUESTION MARKS
12	a person who wants more freedom	**H**	STAIRS
13	someone who tends to be optimistic	**I**	STICK FIGURES
14	a person who is always finding fault with others	**J**	TREES
15	someone who has found the solution to something		
16	a person who is more determined than they appear		
17	someone who accepts the reality of situations		
18	a person who does not say more than is necessary		

Remember to put your answers on the separate answer sheet.

*Read the following magazine article and then answer the questions on page 81. Indicate your answers **on the separate answer sheet**.*

The Organic Farm

In recent years organic farming has made its own impact on the farming community. Encouraged by the general public's awareness of chemical use in the environment, growers are becoming more aware of the demand for organically farmed produce.

Laura Davis grew up in London, far removed from the small country village she later moved to. Although not from an agricultural background, she wasn't impressed by what she had seen of conventional methods. Joining Laurence on the 32 acre smallholding of Bindon Farm provided a perfect opportunity to develop an organic system of farming.

"It was perfect really," she says. "We never considered using chemicals, so we were organic from the start. The land here had never been intensively farmed, it was all permanent pasture, and in the early days it was more an exercise in self-sufficiency than a working farm. Later, when we decided to operate commercially, we both did part-time courses at the local agricultural college. It was a general course, not geared to an organic system.

"There is tremendous confusion about what 'organic' means. We describe organic produce as 'the products of a sustainable system of farming that is environmentally harmless.' In other words, 'organic' describes the system of farming rather than the produce itself. All land has a certain amount of naturally occurring chemicals in it. It's also possible that your produce can be marginally contaminated by, for instance, the farmer next door. So it is wrong to suggest that the product is completely free of chemical residue."

The Soil Association is the body which approves land suitable for organic growing. Their inspectors issue a Soil Association symbol which can be used in the marketing of organic produce. To gain the symbol, land has to be free of chemical use for at least two years – sometimes longer, depending on how it has been used previously. The organic farmer also has to demonstrate competence in organic farming. The Soil Association was in its infancy when Laura and Laurence began and they were among the first to be awarded the symbol.

When they first started operating properly, they were selling to specialist outlets in London. Because they were supplying individually they had to try to meet as many demands as possible. Providing that sort of range and continuity all year round was no easy task. Now they sell their produce via a marketing cooperative, which is a group of 17 growers from various-size farms. Together they plan a crop rotation system. "Forming the cooperative was a logical step," says Laura. "Individual producers were becoming vulnerable as the competition grew amongst themselves, and as the large supermarket chains became more aware of organically produced food. The cooperative has been running for two years now. It is one of the first to try this and to have a national marketing structure. It is a considerable investment for us growers because we fund a full-time manager to control the storage, sales and transport of the produce.

"In some ways we have felt like pioneers. A lot of the work we do has never been done before. There was certainly no pool of knowledge to draw on when we started, so we had to solve our own problems. We made some extremely expensive mistakes but have learned from them and the experience is now useful for helping people who are just coming into the industry. Some of the systems we use return to the traditional rules of farming."

The techniques used by organic growers combine the best of traditional farming with modern methods and it would be a mistake to assume that organic growers are against modern techniques. They use them whenever they can. Machinery is also important to organic farmers, who will adapt what is available to suit the needs of their system.

Planning the rotation of the crops to be grown is vital for Laura and Laurence. Every year in late January they sit down and decide what they will grow and on what area of their land they will grow it. They record this on large maps. It's quite complicated because they have to fit their rotation to that of the other 17 growers. The cooperative will decide they need X amount of potatoes and X amount of onions. They then decide how much of that they can grow. As each participant signs a five-year contract to the cooperative, there is a commitment to the group above personal interest. They hope the interest of the group matches their own.

It's important for them to know in advance that there is a market for what they grow, so that all this careful planning will pay off in the end. It is also necessary for them to spread the planting and harvesting cycle so they don't end up trying to harvest everything at once.

According to Laura, a particular problem organic growers face is in educating the public about the appearance of the produce. ''There seems to be an obsession with cosmetics. Of course, it's much more difficult to get continuity in appearance without using chemicals. We hope that eventually people will pay less attention to the cosmetics and simply appreciate the flavour.''

19   Why did Laura and Laurence start a farm?

   A   They knew organic produce was in demand.
   B   They wanted to grow their own food.
   C   They had trained in organic farming.
   D   They had moved together to the country.

20   According to Laura, the word 'organic' describes

   A   a way of farming that is completely free of chemicals.
   B   a kind of food from which all chemicals have been removed.
   C   a way of growing things without using artificial chemicals.
   D   a kind of food that contains natural but not artificial chemicals.

21   What does the Soil Association do?

   A   It inspects the food grown on organic farms.
   B   It decides whether land is suitable for agriculture.
   C   It inspects the land used by all new farmers.
   D   It decides whether produce can be called organic.

22   When they first started, Laura and Laurence

   A   had difficulty growing enough produce.
   B   weren't sure how much produce to grow.
   C   didn't have enough customers for their produce.
   D   supplied their produce to only one customer.

23   The cooperative was formed

   A   to stop organic farmers competing with each other.
   B   to encourage supermarkets to sell organic produce.
   C   to compete with the produce sold in supermarkets.
   D   to advise people who were starting organic farming.

24   Laura and Laurence plan their year

   A   so that they can harvest at different times from other cooperative members.
   B   according to what kinds of produce they believe there will be a demand for.
   C   so that they can grow different kinds of produce from the previous year.
   D   according to the amounts of produce the cooperative instructs them to grow.

25   According to Laura, the public

   A   should be made more aware of what organic produce is.
   B   find the flavour of organic produce unusual.
   C   expect a certain type of produce to always look the same.
   D   are very concerned about the presence of chemicals in food.

Remember to put your answers on the separate answer sheet.

For questions **26–32**, you must choose which of the paragraphs **A–H** on page **83** match the numbered gaps in the following newspaper article. There is one extra paragraph, which does not belong in any of the gaps. Indicate your answers **on the separate answer sheet**.

Up, up in the air

David Hunn joins a group of balloonists

The sky was not yet light as we assembled for the 20th anniversary of the notorious Icicle Meeting, an assembly of faithful and fanatical balloonists that can prove one of the coldest sporting events of the year.

26	

Ballooning may not strike you as a notably sporting activity and, indeed, there is not a lot of competition about the Icicle Meeting.

27	

The principle of hot-air ballooning is hugely simple. Air expands when it is heated, so there is less weight of it within the balloon than there would be if it were cold air.

28	

The pilot drags the vast sausage of material out of its bag and lays it on the ground, attached to its basket. With a giant fan, he fills it with the air of the day. Propane gas burners are then lit and the heat is drawn in.

29	

Hotter and hotter grows the air within, until the pilot senses the strain that nature is exerting.

30	

Such gentleness attends the ascent of a balloon that it is almost as though sleep still held you in its comfortable grip.

31	

The softest of south-west breezes then drifts us over brown and green fields (there is no steering on these things) and a handful of horses never raise their heads from the grass as we pass by.

From a balloon basket at 200 feet you are privy to some rare sights. The old hands will tell you of rooftop sunbathers taken by surprise and of many a house painter clutching his ladder in alarm.

32	

The pilot then chooses his landing ground – no animals, no crops, no cables, no buildings – and controls the final descent by ripping open a panel to let out the heat that remains in the balloon. Our 69,000 cubic feet comes down and sits as softly on the ground as if we had descended in a lift.

A   There is not much of that in the winter, but country houses can be inspected at leisure and suburban estates lie like so many toy houses at your feet.

B   Then it's hands off and away we go, at the mercy of the wind direction but with altitude at his command: the hotter the higher, the cooler the lower.

C   But it is sporting in the very best of ways, a great gathering of old and young, men and women, whose skill and enthusiasm is focused on one of the loveliest of outdoor activities and who are seldom self-centred enough to decline to help others.

D   Fortune smiled on us that day, though. Although grey and low-clouded, the wind had lost its strength overnight.

E   What they did not know was that it was the heating of the air that provided lift. They thought that smoke itself possessed the properties that produced these magical flights.

F   Your own hot breath puffed into a party balloon has the same effect.

G   Slowly the balloon responds, expanding until it sits up, 80 feet high and 50 feet wide. With the basket now rising into the air, willing hands hold it down and in we climb.

H   And indeed sleep would have been welcome, but ballooning prospers at the beginning of the day, before the ground produces the warm air currents that are the delight of glider pilots.

FOURTH TEXT / QUESTIONS 33–44

Answer questions *33–44* by referring to the magazine article about bees, printed on page *85*. Indicate your answers **on the separate answer sheet**.

Which of the following actions *33–44* has been believed to produce the results listed *A–J*?
Note: Some choices may be required more than once.

33	taking bees across water	A	bees get angry
34	tying fabric to a beehive	B	bees recover from illness
35	using swear words close to bees	C	serious misfortune
36	lifting a beehive as a coffin passes	D	bees die
37	a bee coming into the room	E	bees go away
38	inviting bees to a funeral	F	someone comes to see you
39	arguing a lot in front of bees	G	bees cannot concentrate on their activities
40	forcing a bee out of your home		
41	keeping a bee in a purse	H	someone visits you for a long time
42	turning a beehive round on the owner's death	I	bees continue to be healthy
43	a bee making a noise at a window	J	wealth
44	failing to tell bees the names of a couple getting married		

Remember to put your answers on the separate answer sheet.

BELIEFS ABOUT BEES

Paul Prossart looks at some of the superstitions surrounding bees

You don't find many people these days who would keep a bee in their purse. But catching the first bee seen in the spring was once considered the height of good luck, and if you kept it in your purse, you were certain never to be short of money. Probably because you would be too afraid to open it! This is just one of the many superstitions surrounding bees.

Next time a bee flies in through your window, expect a visitor very shortly. Take a closer look at the bee: if it has a red tail, your visitor will be a man, a white tail means a woman. If the bee happens to be buzzing at the living-room window, make sure there's an ample supply of food – your visitor is probably intending to stay a while. Whatever you do, don't drive the bee out of the house. That would bring incredibly bad luck. Housekeeping would never be the same again.

And were you aware that bees dislike bad behaviour? Years ago, bee-keeping was much more common. A hive or two would provide some honey in the summer months and it wasn't unusual to have a few hives in the back garden. You would never consider owning a hive of bees if your family was quarrelsome. A magazine of the 1850s declared that 'if a man and his wife quarrel, the bees will leave them.'

Bad language should never be used near beehives as it disturbs the bees, affecting their honey-making. Bees, it seems, are paragons of virtue. And make sure you've had a bath if you are going to collect honey from a hive. Bees are fussy about cleanliness. As early as 77AD, Pliny, in his book *Natural History*, advised his readers: 'It is particularly recommended that the person who takes the honey should be well washed and clean.' Bees obviously take a dim view of dirty hands on their pure honey.

They also have mixed feelings where water is concerned because tradition has it that if you move a hive of bees, they must never be taken across a stream or river because they will all die.

There was much concern for bees in the 17th century. It was believed that if the owner of the hives were to die, all the bees would die too, unless they were moved to another place. From this the superstitious custom developed of turning round the beehives that belonged to the deceased, so that the bees would survive.

Once, at the funeral of a rich farmer in the 1790s, someone duly called out to a servant 'Turn the bees', as the body was being placed in the hearse and the horseman was about to pull off in the funeral procession. This servant, having no knowledge of the custom, lifted up the hive and laid it on its side. The bees, naturally, didn't like this, and instantly attacked and fastened onto the horses and riders. The horses bolted and galloped off, with the bees in hot pursuit, and as a mourner commented later: 'A general confusion took place, with loss of hats and wigs.'

By the end of the 19th century, this custom had become a mere lifting of the hives a few inches off the ground as a token gesture whenever a funeral passed the house, as it was still considered necessary for the well-being of the bees.

During that century, when a death occurred, it was thought the done thing to send an invitation to the funeral to the bees in their hives, otherwise they would die. Bees obviously still observe this tradition – and literally, at that – for the *Shrewsbury Chronicle* as recently as 1961 related the story of the death of a beekeeper who was devoted to his bees. At a memorial service in the village, the bees left their hives and settled in a great swarm all over the flowers on their deceased master's grave.

It was the custom at weddings and funerals to give a piece of the wedding cake or funeral biscuit to the bees, telling them the name of the person married or dead. If the bees didn't know of the former they became very annoyed and stung everyone within reach and if they were ignorant of the latter they would become sick and might even die. Why tell them at all, you may wonder!

The tale is told of how, in 1863, a man bought a hive of rather sickly bees at an auction. He had the idea that they had never been put in mourning for their late master's death, so he got a piece of crepe and tied it to a stick, which he fastened to the hive. After this the bees made a full recovery. It became common in the 19th century to see hives of bees with a strip of material tied to them.

So next time you are in the queue at the supermarket and a bee flies out of the purse of the woman in front, don't be surprised – she is just being superstitious.

PAPER 2   WRITING   (2 HOURS)

1   You were recently included in a group of people from your area who were chosen to visit a similar region in Britain, with a view to establishing useful contacts and exchange programmes in education and training. Several weeks after your return, you receive a letter from someone you met in Britain. Here is part of it, together with the newspaper cutting referred to, and part of the programme for your visit.

Read them carefully, and then, **using the information given**, *write the letter described on page 87.*

but some people always manage to get the wrong idea, and now someone has written this silly letter to the local newspaper. I enclose the cutting. I could write a reply myself, but I think it would be better coming from you. You can tell them something about the enormous benefits for us all which might eventually come from this small beginning – and don't forget to point out that so far all the money has come from your people!

How did the photos come out? I seem to have a few good ones of you, which

---

LETTERS TO THE EDITOR

Sir!

I wish to use your columns to register my protest at the recent widely-publicized visit by a foreign delegation of so-called 'students' and 'workers'. While they were here, they seemed to spend most of their time hanging around expensive hotels and restaurants, doubtless at the expense of myself and other local residents. I suppose we paid their plane fares too!

What purpose – other than giving these people a free holiday – was served by such a visit? How will throwing money about like this help our many unemployed young people or bring desperately needed new industry to the area? I suspect that all it will do is provide an opportunity for some of our own greedy and useless citizens to fly off for a free holiday!

In all the many years I have lived in this area, I have never seen such a shocking waste of public money!

Yours, disgusted

Gerald Bell

OUTLINE OF PROGRAMME

MONDAY: *Arrive 11 a.m. Official welcome by Mayor.*
Lunch with representatives of local business and industry.
Afternoon free.
Evening – reception at Regional College.

TUESDAY: *Spend day at company chosen according to interests.*
Lunch-time discussion with trainees and managers.

WEDNESDAY: *Lecture on regional facilities for education and*
vocational training, followed by visit to school or college.
Lunch as guests of representatives of travel and tourism industry.

*Now write **a letter** to the editor of the newspaper, explaining why you think Mr Bell has got the wrong idea about your visit. Describe some of the things you did during your visit, and how they may bring future benefits to the people of the region. You are advised to write approximately 250 words.*

You must lay out the letter in an appropriate way but it is not necessary to include an address.

SECTION B

*Choose **ONE** of the following writing tasks. Your answer should follow exactly the instructions given. Write approximately 250 words.*

2   Here is part of a letter from a reader which has appeared in an international English-language newspaper.

> We have a reputation in Britain for being bad at learning foreign languages, and I must admit that I had no opportunity at all to study a second language when I was at school. I am now in my forties, and I wonder whether it is too late for me to learn another language. So many foreigners speak good English these days, and I would like to ask them two questions. Why are you more successful at learning other languages than we are? Could I study another language successfully at my age?
>
>
>
>   The editor comments: I should like to invite all readers who have experience
>   of learning English to write to us, giving their answers to the two questions.
>   The best three will be printed, and the writers will each receive a small prize.

Write to the editor, **answering the two questions**.

3   An international agency is making a comparability study of working conditions across a range of countries. You have been asked to write a confidential **report** on conditions in the company you work for. You should mention such issues as health and safety at work, pensions, paid holidays, sick-leave and other social benefits provided by the company. Indicate any areas where you feel change is needed.

4   You have been asked to contribute to a guide-book for visitors to your area. Choose **two** of the following topics: sports facilities, the music scene, night-life, eating out, shopping, museums and galleries, entertainments for children, and write your **article** for the guide-book.

5   You recently attended a language course in Britain, which was run by an organization which promised you good tuition and family accommodation. You have no complaints about the tuition, but the accommodation was poor and too far from the school. You feel strongly that the family you stayed with was not a suitable one to place students with. Write **a letter of complaint** to the organization, describing exactly why you were not satisfied with the arrangements.

PAPER 3   ENGLISH IN USE   (1 HOUR 30 MINUTES)

1   *For questions **1–15**, read the text below and then decide which word on page **90** best fits each space. Put the letter you choose for each question in the correct box on your answer sheet. The exercise begins with an example (**0**).*

HOW WE READ

Why did you decide to read this, and will you keep reading to the end? Do you expect to
understand every (**0**) … part of it and will you remember anything about it in a fortnight's
(**1**) … ? Common sense (**2**) … that the answers to these questions depend on "readability" –
whether the (**3**) … matter is interesting, the argument clear and the (**4**) … attractive. But
psychologists are discovering that to (**5**) … why people read – and often don't read –
technical information, they have to (**6**) … not so much the writing as the reader.

Even the most technically confident people often (**7**) … instructions for the video or home
computer in favour of hands-on experience. And people frequently (**8**) … little notice of
consumer information, whether on nutritional labels or in the small print of contracts.
Psychologists researching reading (**9**) … to assume that both beginners and (**10**) … readers
read everything put in front of them from start to finish. There are (**11**) … among them
about the (**12**) … of eyes, memory and brain during the process. Some believe that fluent
readers take (**13**) … every letter or word they see; others (**14**) … that readers rely on
memory or context to carry them from one phrase to another. But they have always assumed
that the reading process is the same: reading starts, comprehension (**15**) … , then reading
stops.

0	**A** absolute	**B** one	**C** single	**D** unique
1	**A** term	**B** period	**C** time	**D** gap
2	**A** suggests	**B** transmits	**C** advises	**D** informs
3	**A** subject	**B** topic	**C** content	**D** text
4	**A** pattern	**B** formation	**C** layout	**D** assembly
5	**A** ensure	**B** determine	**C** value	**D** rate
6	**A** examine	**B** inquire	**C** trace	**D** calculate
7	**A** miss	**B** omit	**C** pass	**D** ignore
8	**A** get	**B** pay	**C** take	**D** make
9	**A** tend	**B** undertake	**C** lead	**D** consent
10	**A** competent	**B** sufficient	**C** considerable	**D** valid
11	**A** objections	**B** arguments	**C** contests	**D** separations
12	**A** role	**B** concern	**C** share	**D** relation
13	**A** up	**B** over	**C** out	**D** in
14	**A** insist	**B** direct	**C** urge	**D** press
15	**A** sets	**B** occurs	**C** issues	**D** establishes

Do not forget to put your answers on the answer sheet.

Example:

2 *For questions **16–30**, complete the following article by writing each missing word on the answer sheet. **Use only one word for each space**. The exercise begins with an example (**0**).*

Trees

All over the world, forests are safeguarding the health of the planet itself. They

do this (**0**) … protecting the soil, providing water and regulating the climate.

Trees bind soil to mountain-sides. Hills where the trees (**16**) … been felled lose

500 times as (**17**) … soil a year as those with trees.

Trees catch and store rainwater. Their leaves break the impact (**18**) … the

rains, robbing (**19**) … of their destructive power. The roots of trees allow the

water (**20**) … go into the soil, which gradually releases (**21**) … to flow down

rivers and refill ground-water reserves. Where (**22**) … are no trees, the rains

run in sheets of water off the land, carrying the soil with them. Land covered

with trees and other plants absorbs 20 times (**23**) … rainwater than bare earth.

As (**24**) … grow, trees absorb carbon dioxide, the main cause of the

'greenhouse effect', (**25**) … threatens irreversibly (**26**) … change the world's

climate. Together, the world's trees, plants and soils contain three times as

much carbon as there (**27**) … in the atmosphere.

The world's forests contain (**28**) … vast majority of its animal and plant species.

The tropical rainforests alone have well (**29**) … half of them, (**30**) … though

they cover only about 6% of the Earth's land surface.

Do not forget to put your answers on the answer sheet.

Example: | ⌐0⌐ | **by** |

91

SECTION B

3 *In **most** lines of the following text, there is **one** word which is **either** grammatically incorrect **or** does not fit in with the sense of the text. For each numbered line **31–44**, find this word and then write it in the space on your answer sheet. Some lines are correct. Indicate these lines with a tick (✓). The exercise begins with two examples (**0**).*

MIDSUMMER IN FINLAND

0   Midsummer, the celebration of the turning of the sun, has been being the

0   highlight of the northern summer for centuries – an event full of symbolism,

31   customs, magic and superstitions. In Finland, Midsummer night is so short

32   as that evening dusk flows into morning dawn almost unnoticed. Even in

33   southern Finland, midnight is the best described as strong twilight.

34   Midsummer night was, the most of all, the celebration of greenery and

35   fruit. Nature is in a full bloom then and the day is never-ending. It was

36   customary throughout Finland to bring branches and greenery to indoors on

37   Midsummer Eve. Houses were so thoroughly cleaned and decorated with

38   birch branches and flower garlands. This 'indoor forest' was complete when

39   leaves on the scrubbed floor gave out a fresh forest aroma. Midsummer is

40   still the Finns' most important one summer celebration. They gather together

41   around the bonfire to make dance, play and be with family and friends

42   themselves. In some areas Midsummer poles decorated with flower garlands and

43   leaves are erected for the festivities. Although some of the old ceremonies are

44   now performed only for fun, Midsummer night, as bathed in the strange

      white light of the North, is still mysterious.

Do not forget to put your answers on the answer sheet.

Examples:

0	being
0	✓

4   *For questions 45–59, read the following formal notice from an employer and use the information to complete the numbered gaps in the informal letter. Then write the new words in the correct spaces on your answer sheet.* **Use no more than two words** *for each gap. The exercise begins with an example (0). The words you need* **do not occur** *in the formal notice.*

FORMAL NOTICE

Academy Bookshop – TERMS OF EMPLOYMENT

1.   Staff must arrive punctually at all times. Anyone persistently arriving late will be dismissed.

2.   Staff must present themselves well-dressed – casual clothing is not permitted.

3.   Staff must make every effort to attend to customers speedily, efficiently and courteously at all times.

4.   Temporary staff should consult a senior member of staff in the event of enquiries to which they are unable to provide an answer.

5.   Temporary staff duties include: taking orders placed by phone; ensuring that orders are prepared prior to customer collection; ensuring that shelves are fully stocked at all times.

6.   Wages are weekly for temporary staff.

INFORMAL LETTER

Dear Mike,

I just thought I'd drop you a line and tell you about the summer job I've just got in a local bookshop. They've just sent me all the rules of the (**0**) … and I must say some of them look a bit strict! I'll (**45**) … get there (**46**) … – that is at 8.30 – and they say that anyone who's (**47**) … will get (**48**) … . We're supposed to be (**49**) … – things like jeans won't (**50**) … . They didn't mention that in the interview!

We're all supposed to (**51**) … to (**52**) … the customers as (**53**) … and as well as we can and we're supposed to be (**54**) … them all the time. Oh and we're supposed to (**55**) … senior if there's a question we can't answer.

It looks as if I'm going to be pretty busy! I'll be taking orders on the phone, getting orders (**56**) … people come to collect them and (**57**) … that the shelves are (**58**) … . Still, they're going to (**59**) … every week, which I'm glad about. Well, I'm not sure if I'm going to enjoy it but it won't be for long and I do need the money.

Hope to see you soon,

Paul

Do not forget to put your answers on the answer sheet.

Example: | 0 | **job** |

SECTION C

5 *For questions **60–65**, read through the following text and then choose from the list **A–K** the best phrase to fill each of the blanks. Write one letter (**A–K**) in the correct box on your answer sheet. **Some of the suggested answers do not fit at all**. One answer has been given as an example (**0**).*

CARD GAME RULES

Card playing has brought pleasure to millions of people for some six centuries and is popular the world over, so it is not surprising to discover that thousands of games have been invented. There is a widespread belief that all card games (**0**) … but the situation is complex and this idea is best ignored. Widely played games (**60**) … in much the same way. National and regional games may have official rules published by an organisation devoted to the game, but these (**61**) … in local and family play. Of course, it is essential to establish a set of rules for club or tournament play, but these (**62**) … as the rules of the club, not the rules of the game. In homes people play cards for enjoyment and (**63**) … and drop rules to suit their tastes. It is because tastes (**64**) … and generation to generation that card games evolve. Games that no longer evolve become extinct.

No book can do more than (**65**) … , or are said by other books to be played. Nor should it expect to. The only important thing is that everybody playing around the same table at the same time should be following the same rules.

A played in its country of origin

B should be regarded

C will naturally introduce

D have decided between alternative rules

E tend to be played everywhere

F never did lay down official rules

G vary from place to place

H describe how games are played

J are happily ignored

K have official rules

Do not forget to put your answers on the answer sheet.

Example: 0 | K

6 *Use the following notes to write about the aeroplane, Concorde. Write in* **complete sentences** *on the back of Answer Sheet Two for each numbered set of notes, using connecting words and phrases as appropriate.* **Write only one sentence for each set of notes.** *You may add words or change the form of the words given in the notes but do not add any extra information. The first point has been expanded for you as an example.*

<table>
<tr><td colspan="2" align="center">CONCORDE</td></tr>
<tr><td>0</td><td>First successful supersonic airliner, passenger services; described 'ultimate flying experience'</td></tr>
<tr><td>81</td><td>Developed 1950s, result of cooperation Britain/France; distinctive shape (bird-like)</td></tr>
<tr><td>82</td><td>First flight Mar 1969; became first supersonic airliner in commercial service, Jan 1976</td></tr>
<tr><td>83</td><td>Length: 70m; wing span: 29 m; capacity: max 100 passengers</td></tr>
<tr><td>84</td><td>Speed: 2x speed of sound (first achieved 1970)</td></tr>
<tr><td>85</td><td>Operators: British Airways, Air France; destinations: incl. London→New York/Miami; Paris→New York.</td></tr>
<tr><td>86</td><td>Special flights: e.g., trips → Lapland (Christmas period), trips → Cairo, Moscow, Vienna; day trips London → Paris</td></tr>
<tr><td>87</td><td>Flight time London → New York: average: 3 hrs 40 mins; record: (set Apr 1990) 2 hrs 55 minutes</td></tr>
<tr><td>88</td><td>For passengers: seats, soft leather; 1 member of crew/16 passengers; meal (5-course); free gift</td></tr>
</table>

The space on page 96 can be used for your rough answers.

Do not forget to put your answers on the back of Answer Sheet Two.

0   *Concorde is the first successful supersonic airliner to be used on passenger services and has been described as 'the ultimate flying experience'.*

81

82

83

84

85

86

87

88

PAPER 4   LISTENING   (APPROX. 45 MINUTES)

*You will hear part of a talk about the ring-pull can, the container in which many drinks are sold. For questions **1–12**, fill in the missing details.*
You will hear the recording twice.

The Ring-Pull Can

Reasons why popular: *completely safe*

| 1 | | *to make* |

easy to open

never | 2 |

not harmful to the environment

Thickness of can surface: | 3 |

Depth of cut in surface: | 4 |

Requirements: *Must break* | 5 |

Must be | 6 |

Size of cut   *Must not be* | 7 | *or*

| 8 |

Unsuitable shapes of cut: | 9 | *and*

| 10 |

Reason why two stages of opening: | 11 |

Cost of making each one: | 12 |

SECTION B

*You will hear part of a radio programme in which future events are discussed. For questions **13–20**, indicate whether the statements are made about each event by writing **YES** or **NO** in the box provided.*

Listen very carefully because you will hear the recording only ONCE.

WHAT'S ON THIS WEEKEND

HIGHFIELD CARNIVAL

It ends quite early.	13	
It is well-known in other countries.	14	
Local people still take part in it.	15	

FRANKTON ROCK FESTIVAL

| It hasn't been held for a long time. | 16 | |
| There will be no well-known groups. | 17 | |

THE OPERA

It has never been performed before	18	
It is likely to be well-attended.	19	
Tickets are very expensive.	20	

SECTION C

You will hear part of an interview with an explorer. For questions 21–30, complete the sentences.
You will hear the piece twice.

The Explorer

It could be said that his expeditions over the last five years have mostly

21 [_____] but there have been **22** [_____]

on any of them.

He thinks that **23** [_____] of his expeditions has been good

and

that **24** [_____] and **25** [_____] have been

right. One of the aims of his expedition to Antarctica is to raise money for a

26 [_____] .

The second aim is to find out what the human body can tolerate when working

very hard and **27** [_____] in extreme temperatures.

These days he does not emphasise **28** [_____] involved in

exploring because people don't take it seriously.

He intends to go to **29** [_____] this year.

On the next expedition to Antarctica they are taking special sledges and

30 [_____] than on the previous expedition there.

PAPER 1 READING (1 HOUR + 15 MINUTES)

FIRST TEXT / QUESTIONS 1–8

*For questions **1–8**, you must choose which of the paragraphs **A–I** on page **103** match the numbered gaps in the following record sleeve notes. There is one extra paragraph, which does not belong in any of the gaps. Indicate your answers **on the separate answer sheet.***

BIG BILL BROONZY

In the vast field of American folk-blues music there have been few figures who have exerted the powerful shaping influences that emanated from Big Bill Broonzy during his lifetime.

1

He was additionally an unbelievably talented composer, and his organising influence and genius in recording sessions will undoubtedly bear closer examination and analysis in years to come. Highly regarded by all his associates, in fact by all individuals having even a cursory interest in his art form, his performances were always of the highest musical and creative standards. On top of this, his attitudes toward his contemporary artists of equal or lesser stature are well known.

2

Big Bill was born William Lee Conley Broonzy in Scott, Mississippi. His birth date is uncertain, as was quite usual with many others of his generation. Bill himself gave it as about 1893. His sister claimed that June 26, 1898 was the correct date.

3

A fiddle of the home-made, cigar-box variety was his first instrument and he also played mandolin in his early years. At the tender age of fourteen he was regularly playing and performing at picnics. As a young man he served in the Army during the First World War, and shortly after his return he left Arkansas for Chicago, where he fell heavily into the blues scene of that city. It was quite a scene too.

4

It was a usual occurrence to have Bill, along with such people as Tampa Red, Sonny Boy Williamson and Washboard Sam and numerous others playing at such a gathering, and during this time, Bill's influence was felt by virtually all who came into contact with him. He was the main participant in hundreds of recording sessions and at other times he was the organising force behind the sessions of other artists and took part as an assisting artist.

5

In 1939, he took part in the now legendary "Spirituals to Swing" concert at Carnegie Hall. He was a tremendous hit, termed by some "unforgettable", and it appears that the potentially awesome nature of the famous auditorium inspired him to perform as strongly as he would have had the event been a house-rent party.

6

In the 1940s, he was continually active in and around his adopted hometown of Chicago, with records and personal appearances. In the 1950s, he made two trips to Europe for concerts, where he encountered a tremendous reception.

7

During his lifetime Big Bill, despite his indisputable musical abilities, was unable to depend totally upon his music to sustain himself. As was and still is the case with all too many musical talents, the return for his efforts was by no means commensurate with his artistry.

8

His death came on August 14, 1958 and his obituary and tributes appeared in a wide variety of newspapers and publications throughout the world. All of this served to emphasise the greatness of this near-legendary musical figure.

A Critical reception of this performance was uniformly excellent and his exceptional talent was observed and realised by many listeners for the first time. It was a memorable occasion in Broonzy's life, as it must have been to those in attendance.

B Broonzy was always the first to offer aid or assistance in most any way, whether it was to compose a song for an individual, to give him or her musical instruction, to afford his services as accompanying musician or perhaps to merely bolster the confidence of an aspiring, struggling artist.

C At any rate, he was one of a vast brood of seventeen children born of parents who first saw the light of day in slavery. He appears to have acquired a great deal of his musical skill, and numerous songs, from one of his uncles. His formative years were spent in Arkansas.

D Following this, he continued playing guitar for as long as he was physically able, his health rapidly deteriorating during this period of time. Fate, playing its cruel hand, had decreed that Bill should no longer be capable of singing, depriving him of what had been his life's blood.

E Whatever his status was at each of these, his overwhelming influence was always felt, his individual stamp and qualities being obvious on recordings much too numerous to mention.

F He was possessed of a great many varied talents: he was a magnificent guitarist, both as soloist and accompanist; a singer of all types of song falling within the black experience – spirituals, blues, work songs, folk material; and a superb storyteller.

G This undeserved plight required him, at various times, to become a porter, gang labourer, cook, caretaker, floor mopper and foundry worker, a not-unusual history for individuals performing in Bill's particular field. By some standards, Bill may have been considered a rather fortunate artist because he was such a frequent visitor to recording studios but, despite this fact, it is all too obvious that his wonderful talent and abilities were not enough to enable him to be a full-time music maker.

H It appears that the people overseas were far more familiar with, and appreciative of, Bill's several and varied musical talents. In addition, his human warmth, charisma and general gregariousness made a distinct and lasting impression upon all who came into contact with him.

I The popularity of house-rent parties was at its height at this time, the purpose of such undertakings being the raising of rent for a particular individual, accompanied by a cacophony of music and good times.

Remember to put your answers on the separate answer sheet.

SECOND TEXT / QUESTIONS 9–19

*Answer questions **9–19** by referring to the magazine article about household goods, printed on page **105**. Indicate your answers **on the separate answer sheet**.*

According to the article, for which household goods are the following statements true? Choose your answers from the list of household goods, **A–G**.

Note: When more than one answer is required, these may be given **in any order**.
    Some choices may be required more than once.

One of the advantages of them is how tough they are.

9 . . . .

Something has been added to them to make them more attractive.

10 . . . .

Some were considered unreliable when they first came out.

11 . . . . .12 . . . .

They are made from something that previously had a completely different use.

13 . . . .

They were widely used before the 1950s.

14 . . . . .15 . . . . .16 . . . .

The form in which they were sold changed in the 1950s.

17 . . . .

Methods used before their invention now sound unpleasant.

18 . . . .

They are considered to have a serious disadvantage.

19 . . . .

A	TOILET CLEANERS
B	DISHWASHERS
C	PLASTIC BAGS
D	FRIDGES
E	VACUUM CLEANERS
F	NON-STICK PANS
G	WASHING-UP LIQUIDS

Remember to put your answers on the separate answer sheet.

HOUSEHOLD GOODS

NON-STICK PANS

The non-stick surface was originally used for coating nose-cone heat shields on spacecraft. Polytetrafluoroethylene (PTFE), its chemical name, was actually discovered by Dupont in the 1940s. It was in the 1950s, however, that a French chemist, Monsieur Gregoire, found a way of applying PTFE to a pan and thus Tefal was born. Now, 70% of cookware is non-stick.

FRIDGES

Cellars, larders and food-preserving methods like smoking, salting and sterilising played a part in keeping food fresh before fridges. Despite their climate, it was the Swedes who were the first to use compressed gas to keep things cold. Britain first saw the fridge in the mid-1920s. At the time it was said that "tests demonstrate it is a mistake to procure too cheap or too small a fridge, as they are seldom efficiently insulated and the cost of running is high." The fridge was deemed a luxury in Britain until well into the 1950s and freezers weren't sold there until 1956.

TOILET CLEANERS

Once upon a time, toilets were cleaned with spirits of salt and hydrochloric acid. Then, in the 1920s, British scientist Harry Pickup began selling white waste powder from factories as a way of cleaning toilets. Eager for immortality, he combined the first three letters of his names and called the product Harpic. He went on to market an explosive drain cleaner called Sanpic, after his wife Sandra Pickup and an ointment called Respic, after the rest of the Pickup family. Harpic went on to become Britain's leading toilet cleaner in the 1940s and 1950s, its formulation unchanged until the 1960s, when a perfume was introduced to increase its appeal.

VACUUM CLEANERS

Designed by GWG Ferris, the man who also gave us the fairground big wheel, vacuum cleaners were in fact invented at the turn of the century. But their high price and running cost made them too expensive for most until the late 1920s, when they became affordable for many. Until then, wealthy households called in a man who brought along the apparatus and cleaned the house.

PLASTIC BAGS

Though the plastic bag was invented in the 1930s, it was not until the 1960s, when plastic quality had improved and seams could be depended upon, that it rivalled the paper bag in popularity. Launched then as a gimmick to encourage impulse buying, it wasn't long before every supermarket was selling (or giving away) this symbol of the throwaway society. Now, large chains hand out around 700 million plastic carriers each year and, according to a recent survey, 51% of British shoppers use new bags every time. Plastic bags have the edge over paper ones on strength and durability, but lose points because they are made from oil, a diminishing resource. Supermarkets now urge shoppers to re-use plastic bags or take along their own shopping bags.

WASHING-UP LIQUIDS

Would you care to sink your hands into ashes to clean greasy plates or use sand and brick dust to remove stubborn dirt? These were among the predecessors of washing-up liquid. The nearest equivalent to our modern version was household soap in a muslin bag, rubbed onto the dish or pot.

The first commercially successful washing-up liquid was introduced in the 1940s, in glass bottles. Then, in the 1950s, plastic containers took over. Now, a family of four uses twenty 500ml bottles of washing-up liquid each year. The contents are rather more sophisticated than dust and ashes and many now use environmentally-friendly ingredients such as palm oil.

DISHWASHERS

The dishwasher existed in the 1920s, when it consisted of a tub with a basket for crockery and a propeller to churn water. The first automatic dishwasher came out in the 1960s and it was from then that it caught on. A modern dishwasher saves the average family 25 minutes a day and its running costs are favourable.

THIRD TEXT / QUESTIONS 20–37

*Read the following public announcement and then answer the questions on page **108**. Indicate your answers **on the separate answer sheet**.*

PRESS COMPLAINTS COMMISSION
CODE OF PRACTICE

All members of the press have a duty to maintain the highest professional and ethical standards. In doing so, they should have regard to the provisions of this code of practice and to safeguarding the public's right to know.

Editors are responsible for the actions of journalists employed by their publications. They should also satisfy themselves as far as possible that material was obtained in accordance with this code.

A

- Newspapers and periodicals should take care not to publish inaccurate, misleading or distorted material.
- Whenever it is recognised that a significant inaccuracy, misleading statement or distorted report has been published, it should be corrected promptly and with due prominence.
- An apology should be published whenever appropriate.

B　Opportunity to reply

- A fair opportunity for reply to inaccuracies should be given to individuals or organisations when reasonably called for.

C　Comment, conjecture and fact

- Newspapers, whilst free to be partisan, should distinguish clearly between comment, conjecture and fact.

D

- Intrusions and enquiries into an individual's private life without his or her consent are not generally acceptable and publication can only be justified when in the public interest. This would include: detecting or exposing crime or serious misdemeanour; detecting or exposing seriously anti-social conduct; protecting public health and safety; preventing the public from being misled by some statement or action of that individual.

E　Hospitals

- Journalists or photographers making enquiries at hospitals or similar institutions should identify themselves to a responsible official and obtain permission before entering non-public areas.
- The restrictions on intruding into privacy are particularly relevant to inquiries about individuals in hospitals or similar institutions.

F　Misrepresentation

- Journalists should not generally obtain or seek to obtain information or pictures through misrepresentation or trickery.
- Unless in the public interest, documents or photographs should be removed only with the express consent of the owner.
- Trickery can be justified only in the public interest and only when material cannot be obtained by any other means.
- In all these clauses, the public interest is defined as in D above.

G

- Journalists should neither obtain nor seek to obtain information or pictures through intimidation.
- Unless their inquiries are in the public interest, journalists should not photograph individuals or private property without their consent, should not persist in telephoning or questioning individuals after having been asked to leave, and should not follow them.
- The public interest is as in D above.

H

- Payments or offers of payment for stories, pictures or information should not be made to witnesses or potential witnesses in current criminal proceedings or to people engaged in crime or to their associates except where the material concerned ought to be published in the public interest and the payment is necessary for this to be done. The public interest is defined in D above.
- "Associates" include family, friends, neighbours and colleagues.
- Payments should not be made either directly or indirectly through agents.

I	Intrusion into grief or shock

- In cases involving personal grief or shock, inquiries should be carried out and approaches made with sympathy and discretion.

J	Innocent relatives and friends

- The Press should generally avoid identifying relatives or friends of persons convicted or accused of crime unless the reference to them is necessary for the full, fair and accurate reporting of the crime or legal proceedings.

K	

- The Press should avoid prejudicial or pejorative reference to a person's race, colour, religion or sex or to any physical or mental illness or handicap.
- It should avoid publishing details of a person's race, colour, religion or sex unless these are directly relevant to the story.

L	Financial journalism

- Even where the law does not prohibit it, journalists should not use for their own profit financial information they receive in advance of its general publication, nor should they pass such information to others.
- They should not write about shares or securities in whose performance they know that they or their close families have a significant financial interest, without disclosing the interest to the editor or financial editor.
- They should not buy or sell, either directly or through nominees or agents, shares or securities about which they have written recently or about which they intend to write in the near future.

M	Confidential sources

- Journalists have a moral obligation to protect confidential sources of information.

For questions **20–32**, answer by choosing from the sections of the article **A–M**.
Note: When more than one answer is required, these may be given **in any order**.
Some of the sections may be chosen more than once.

Which section refers to:

journalists giving personal opinions in articles?	20 ....
investigating illegal acts?	21 ....
interviewing people in a considerate way?	22 ....
reporting on court cases?	23 .... 24 ....
getting permission to take people's personal property away?	25 ....
naming people who give information to journalists?	26 ....
journalists using information for personal gain?	27 ....
people denying stories that have been written?	28 ....
information affecting journalists' relatives?	29 ....
journalists who keep pursuing people?	30 ....
giving information about people that is unconnected with the story?	31 .... 32 ....

For questions **33–37**, choose the most suitable headings for the following sections of the article from the list **A–H** below.

33	Section A	**A**	Apologies
34	Section D	**B**	Pressurizing people
35	Section G	**C**	Using official information
36	Section H	**D**	Accuracy
37	Section K	**E**	Discrimination
		F	Privacy
		G	Identification
		H	Deals for articles

Remember to put your answers on the separate answer sheet.

*Read the following magazine article and then answer the questions on page 110. Indicate your answers **on the separate answer sheet**.*

VOLUNTARY SERVICE OVERSEAS

VSO (Voluntary Service Overseas) was always a great idea for people in their 20s, but what is less commonly known is that older volunteers are especially welcome. Today's volunteer force includes many professions – teachers, nurses, midwives, boat-builders, physiotherapists, architects, solicitors and food technologists. Volunteers are aged between 20 and 70 – the average age is 33. There are roughly equal numbers of men and women and the great majority are single. However, between 15 and 20 per cent of the volunteer force is made up of couples.

VSO aims to relieve poverty by sending volunteers on two-year placements to work alongside people in less developed countries. Unlike other charities, VSO sends people, not money, to the country in need. It has been described as an organisation that cares about the unequal distribution of material goods and opportunities in the world and, as former VSO director Neil McIntosh says, "VSO means caring about others – knowing that their deprivation diminishes us." Since the first volunteers trekked out 30 years ago, more than 19,000 volunteers have now worked throughout Africa, Asia, the Caribbean and the Pacific, training the local workforce in vital skills.

For many people, VSO conjures up images of enthusiastic volunteers disappearing for two years into poverty-stricken areas, far from any form of civilisation. But as VSO Operations Director Brian Rockliffe explains, the reality can be very different. "Many do end up working in places with no electricity or running water but, equally, many are allocated jobs in an environment similar to one back home. For example, some find work in a capital city, while others are employed in a university or clinic."

So how are volunteers selected? Competition for the 750 places on offer each year is fierce – every day the VSO offices receive hundreds of enquiries from potential applicants. For this reason, VSO has introduced a rigorous selection procedure. This is deliberately testing, for VSO is not an easy option for drop-outs who fancy working abroad – the quality of volunteer is vital. The 8-page application form is the first stage of the application process. Next comes a one-day assessment, in which groups of applicants are put through tests to measure their motivation and ability to work well with others. Those accepted also go on a post-selection training and briefing weekend. Qualities looked for include adaptability, flexibility, open-mindedness and a willingness to learn. But the selection process isn't infallible and, despite its rigours, ten per cent of volunteers return home within nine months. Obviously, some return because of things going wrong back home, but a proportion find they just can't take the lifestyle.

Most volunteers are sent out within six months of being accepted. Most are happy to go to any developing country and the more flexible they are, the sooner they will go. Each volunteer is given three grants – one before going, to equip him or herself, another to help settle in, and a final 're-equipment' grant on return to this country. VSO sorts out work permits, pays National Insurance for volunteers and offers a scheme to compensate for loss of pension earnings. Salaries, which are generally intended to cover only basic living, are paid by the government of the host country, although in some cases these are so low that VSO supplements them. Outward and return flights are paid for by VSO and accommodation is found and paid for by the volunteer's employers abroad.

Some volunteers stay for a third year and some marry while abroad and never come back. But the vast majority return home, though it's not necessarily very easy to settle back into life back at home, as ex-volunteer Craig explains. "It's so difficult to share your experiences with others. They express an interest and ask you to talk about it but they're not really interested because they can't relate to it." For this reason many volunteers stay in contact with each other after returning. "That's also why couples who go together find it such a great experience," says Craig, "because they have so many shared memories to talk about."

VSO is definitely very hard work but the great plus is that, as well as having your own memories, your work can be said to have real, long-term results. So, who knows, maybe you could do it. You never know until you try …

38   When recruiting volunteers, VSO looks for

    A   young single people.
    B   equal numbers of men and women.
    C   people of any age.
    D   people from specific professions.

39   Which of the following statements best sums up the thinking behind VSO?

    A   Too little money is given to less developed countries.
    B   People in less developed countries cannot help themselves.
    C   The problems of less developed countries affect everyone.
    D   Other charities ignore some countries that need help.

40   In what way is VSO work different from most people's impression of it?

    A   Volunteers are generally not sent to the very poor areas.
    B   Conditions may be worse than is generally expected.
    C   Volunteers can generally choose to go to areas they prefer.
    D   Conditions may be more familiar than is generally expected.

41   What kind of people does the selection process aim to eliminate?

    A   people who are volunteering because of problems at home
    B   people who have never worked in teams before
    C   people who are not physically fit enough
    D   people who see it as an opportunity to spend time overseas

42   VSO always pays for everything except

    A   accommodation.
    B   basic living costs.
    C   flights.
    D   personal equipment.

43   What often happens to volunteers on returning home?

    A   Other people feel that they have changed.
    B   They can no longer get on with other people at home.
    C   Other people pay little attention to their stories.
    D   They get irritated by questions about their experiences.

Remember to put your answers on the separate answer sheet.

PAPER 2 WRITING (2 HOURS)

1   You have been told that you must improve your English, but you also want to have a good holiday abroad and practise plenty of sports. One day you find an advert for sports holidays in New Zealand, which seems to be exactly what you want. At the same time, you receive a letter and cutting from Peggy Milne, an old friend of your family.

*Read the letter and advertisements carefully, and then, **using the information given**, write the two letters listed below.*

For young sportsmen and women, wherever you come from, **Southern Star Holidays** offer

THE SPORTS HOLIDAY OF A LIFETIME

in New Zealand's beautiful South Island

Full range of activities – all the way from hiking to bungee-jumping!

Optional English-language tuition available every morning

Basic accommodation arranged at reasonable cost

SOUTH ISLAND INTENSIVE LANGUAGE COURSES

Long-established as the place for best results and exam success.

Small classes and expert tuition, whatever your level. Classes take place from 9 to 12 and 2 to 4.30 each day, with a range of optional evening activities.

Accommodation in local families can be arranged for you, and

We are hoping you will come and visit us this year, especially as we hear that you need to improve your English. You'd certainly have every chance to do that here!

I enclose details of an intensive course, which I could easily arrange for you to do. The college is quite near here, and of course we should love to have you to stay. We have plenty of room, especially now Vicky and Jenny have both left home to work elsewhere. Roy and I would both enjoy having a young person around the house again, and hearing all the latest news about your family.

Do get in touch soon. We look forward to hearing from you.

Yours

Peggy

P.S. Roy sends his regards to all the family.

Now write

a   *a letter to Mrs Milne, thanking her for her suggestions, but explaining that you will probably make other plans (write about 150 words)*

b   *a letter to Southern Star Holidays, asking for further details of cost and accommodation, and more precise information about the English-language tuition they offer (write about 100 words)*

You must lay out your letters in an appropriate way but it is not necessary to include addresses.

SECTION B

*Choose **ONE** of the following writing tasks. Your answer should follow exactly the instructions given. Write approximately 250 words.*

2   English-speaking holidaymakers who visit your country sometimes get into difficult situations because they don't know enough about local customs. The Tourist Information Office in your town has asked you to prepare **a leaflet** in English, explaining the things foreign visitors ought to know about your way of life, and advising them of anything they should remember to do or not to do.

3   An American college student is shortly going to spend three months at your school, college or workplace, as part of the course she is taking. You have been chosen as the person who will meet the student and help her to settle in. Write her **a letter** in which you introduce yourself, give the details of her arrival, accommodation and programme, and give any advice or information you think she will need to have before arrival.

4   An international market research company has asked you to contribute to a study of television services in a number of different countries. Write **a report** on television in your country, commenting on the degree of choice available, and on programme quality. Mention anything you would like to see changed in future, and any aspects of the service you particularly like.

5   The Principal of the Language Institute where you study English has put this note up on the main notice-board.

> **ENGLISH LANGUAGE SECTION OF LIBRARY**
>
> I am keen to improve this section of the library, and would welcome your participation in the process. All students of English in this college can help me by doing the following:
>
> Write up to 250 words about **ONE** book (fact or fiction, as long as it is in English) which you would like to suggest we buy for the library. Please include details of:
>
> a   **what the book is about**
> b   **why you like it**
> c   **what kinds of people you think will enjoy it**
>
> Two more points to bear in mind: our students come from a wide variety of age-groups and backgrounds; we are not planning to buy any more English-language textbooks for the library.
>
> I look forward to reading your suggestions.

Write about the book you would like to suggest for the library.

PAPER 3   ENGLISH IN USE   (1 HOUR 30 MINUTES)

1 *For questions **1–15**, read the text below and then decide which word on page **114** best fits each space. Put the letter you choose for each question in the correct box on your answer sheet. The exercise begins with an example (**0**).*

The Body Clock

Scientists used to believe that our 24-hour cycle of sleeping and waking was (**0**) … entirely by external factors. The most notable of these, they thought, were the rising and (**1**) … of the sun. But they have now (**2**) … that there is a daily rhythm to a (**3**) … range of biological functions – including temperature, digestion and mental (**4**) … – which are regulated internally by a special time-keeping mechanism within the brain.

The main function of this 'body clock' is to anticipate and (**5**) … for external changes so that, for example, our body temperature starts to rise (**6**) … dawn, gearing us up for the day, and begins to (**7**) … in the early evening, winding us down for sleep.

Some people's body clocks (**8**) … poorer time than others, which can greatly disturb their lives and even (**9**) … their health. Insomnia, depression, fatigue, poor work performance and even accidents can all be (**10**) … or aggravated by inaccurate body clocks.

(**11**) … severe problems can result from the difficulties of (**12**) … to different time zones and working by night instead of by day. Shift workers are known to run a higher-than-average (**13**) … of having a number of health problems and the disruption of (**14**) … body rhythms is one possible (**15**) … for this.

0	**A** conducted	**B** steered	**C** governed	**D** managed
1	**A** descending	**B** diving	**C** plunging	**D** setting
2	**A** established	**B** fixed	**C** settled	**D** assured
3	**A** wide	**B** various	**C** far	**D** grand
4	**A** operation	**B** activity	**C** process	**D** occupation
5	**A** dispose	**B** scheme	**C** steady	**D** prepare
6	**A** beside	**B** approximately	**C** around	**D** nearly
7	**A** fall	**B** reduce	**C** lessen	**D** subtract
8	**A** keep	**B** hold	**C** support	**D** preserve
9	**A** risk	**B** spoil	**C** injure	**D** threaten
10	**A** put	**B** formed	**C** caused	**D** made
11	**A** Parallel	**B** Equally	**C** Alike	**D** Compared
12	**A** altering	**B** adjusting	**C** fitting	**D** suiting
13	**A** risk	**B** danger	**C** threat	**D** hazard
14	**A** common	**B** conditional	**C** normal	**D** used
15	**A** explanation	**B** solution	**C** account	**D** source

Do not forget to put your answers on the answer sheet.

Example:

2   *For questions **16–30**, complete the following article by writing each missing word on the answer sheet. **Use only one word for each space**. The exercise begins with an example (**0**).*

Chess Tournaments

All tournament chess games are played with a chess clock – that (**0**) … , two clocks joined together. When one player makes his move, he presses a button (**16**) … stops his clock and starts his opponent's clock. (**17**) … fails to keep to the time limit, no (**18**) … what the position on the board, loses the game. Weekend tournaments with a fast time limit and long sessions of play of (**19**) … to twelve hours a day are very strenuous and result (**20**) … fatigue and time troubles. The play is quite sharp. Active, attacking chess (**21**) … the order of the day and it is difficult to maintain (**22**) … sustained, precise defence against such play. A score of the game must be kept as play goes on. Each move is written (**23**) … on a score sheet, which (**24**) … to be handed to the tournament officials at the end of each round. The only thought in everyone's head is (**25**) … win. Talent and youth – that's (**26**) … is needed for success at chess, with the emphasis (**27**) … youth. Some approach the board with a slow, purposeful manner (**28**) … giving you a second glance – you simply don't count. They seem to imply that (**29**) … outcome is a foregone conclusion for them; you only (**30**) … to accept it with good grace.

Do not forget to put your answers on the answer sheet.

Example: | 0 | **is** |

115

SECTION B

3   In **most** lines of the following text, there is **either** a spelling **or** a punctuation error. For each numbered line **31–43**, write the correctly spelled word(s) or show the correct punctuation in the spaces on your answer sheet. Some lines are correct. Indicate these lines with a tick (✓). The exercise begins with three examples (**0**).

AMERICAN INDIANS

0   Since the early Nineteenth century, the number of published accounts

0   of the openning of the American West has risen into the thousands.

0   The greatest concentration of recorded experience and observation came

31   out of the thirty year period between 1860 and 1890, an incredible era

32   of violense, greed, audacity and sentimentality. During that time, the

33   culture and way of life of the American Indian was destroyed and out

34   of that time came virtually all the great tails of the American West.

35   Only occassionally was the voice of an Indian heard. Yet they are not

36   all lost those Indian voices of the past. A few authentic accounts of

37   this important period of American history were recorded by Indians.

38   Newspaper reporters frequently interviewed warriors and chiefs and

39   gave them the oportunity to express their opinions on what was

40   happening. The quality of these interviews varyed greatly, depending

41   upon the wilingness of the Indians to speak freely or upon each

42   interpreters abilities. The Indians depended on imagery to express their

43   thoughts. With a good interpreter, an Indians words could be made to

        sound poetic but with a poor interpreter they might sound flat.

Do not forget to put your answers on the answer sheet.

Examples:

0	nineteenth
0	opening
0	✓

4   *For questions 44–58, read the following informal note about starting a college Film Society and use the information to complete the numbered gaps in the formal announcement. Then write the new words in the correct spaces on your answer sheet.* **Use no more than two words** *for each gap. The exercise begins with an example (0). The words you need* **do not occur** *in the informal note.*

INFORMAL NOTE

Do you think you could come up with some sort of notice about the Film Club we decided should be started in the committee meeting the other day? Since you were made the organiser of it, it's best that you let everyone know about it.

Obviously, the fact that so many people have said they want a club like this is the main reason why we've decided to set it up. So make it clear that we're doing it because of that. Since we didn't have any strong idea ourselves about which particular films we should show, mention that you'd be glad of any suggestions. Don't forget to mention that we've decided the club should meet every week and that they won't have to pay to join. But make sure that you point out that they'll have to pay a small amount for each screening – just enough to pay for the films and equipment we have to hire. Oh, and don't forget to mention that they can get things like ice-cream and cold drinks while the film's on. And get them to sign a list if they want to join.

Regards,

Janet

FORMAL ANNOUNCEMENT

It was decided at the (**0**) ... committee meeting that a college Film Society is to be (**44**) ... and I have been (**45**) ... its organiser. The committee was aware of the (**46**) ... such a club that many of you have expressed and it is in (**47**) ... this that the decision has been taken.

As the committee have no (**48**) ... regarding the exact (**49**) ... the films we will be showing, I would (**50**) ... any suggestions that you might make. It is (**51**) ... that the society will meet on a (**52**) ... and that (**53**) ... will be made for (**54**) .... There will, however, be a small charge for each screening to (**55**) ... costs of film and equipment hire.

Screenings will take place in the Central Hall and a selection of (**56**) ... will be (**57**) ....

(**58**) ... to join should sign below.

Alan Hudson

Do not forget to put your answers on the answer sheet.

Example: | 0 | **recent** |

SECTION C

5   *For questions **59–64**, read through the following text and then choose from the list **A–K** the best phrase to fill each of the blanks. Write one letter (**A–K**) in the correct box on your answer sheet. **Some of the suggested answers do not fit at all**. One answer has been given as an example (**0**).*

FILM COMPANY TRADEMARKS

Trademark designs – or logos – identifying film companies have been around since cinema's early days. In the era of silent films, viewers looked for the name of the company before they looked for who the stars were and they were rarely interested in the director. (**0**) … by many film companies and it was an important part of each studio's publicity. (**59**) … and quite detailed accounts survive concerning some of them.

(**60**) … since the original company was founded. The image was taken from a childhood memory of a mountain in Utah, where its founder grew up, while the title was borrowed from the name of a construction site down the road from his office.

(**61**) … but was soon redesigned into the form we would recognise today. (**62**) … but the company soon returned to it, coloured blue and orange and floating in front of a blue sky. Logos that feature blue skies form a kind of species within the field of film company trademarks, with Warner Brothers, Columbia and Paramount all using it as a background. (**63**) … – they all want to be the greatest and the largest and to become part of the everyday landscape.

(**64**) … and their logo also features the sky in another sense – seeing it all from outer space. It has gone through many transformations, with the early orbiting plane being replaced by the famous mirrored globe.

A   It was abandoned briefly in the 1970s

B   A young executive was given the task of creating a memorable trademark

C   The version with which we are familiar now was introduced in 1924

D   Universal certainly chose their name for this reason

E   Perhaps this reflects the domineering aspirations of film companies

F   The Warner Brothers trademark began life as a rather austere shield

G   The trademarks which we would recognise today have undergone many transformations over the years

H   Paramount's snowy peak has survived virtually unchanged

J   Occasionally film makers have even made inventive use of these trademarks

K   The logo was used at the start of every film

Do not forget to put your answers on the answer sheet.

Example: `0`   **K**

6 *Use the following notes to write about McDonald's, the food company. Write in* **complete sentences** *on the back of Answer Sheet Two for each numbered set of notes, adding connecting words and phrases as appropriate.* **Write only one sentence for each set of notes.** *You may add words and change the form of the words given in the notes but do not add any extra information. The first point has been expanded for you as an example.*

McDONALD'S

0	*Chain, fast food restaurants; worldwide*
81	*Founder Ray Kroc; idea from small stall, California (name 'McDonald's Hamburgers') run by two brothers (Mac & Dick McDonald)*
82	*First restaurant: outdoors, Chicago, 1955 (hamburgers, fries, milkshakes)*
83	*1963: 500th restaurant; new products; income over $1m*
84	*1967: first indoor restaurants + first restaurants outside US; first nationwide TV ads shown (US)*
85	*1971: restaurants Japan, Australia, Germany, etc; McDonald's in every US state*
86	*Breakfast food: started 1977 (later served 25% all breakfasts eaten outside home, US)*
87	*1984: 18m customers per day (equivalent lunch for entire pop. Australia and New Zealand)*
88	*1990: 100+ hamburgers every second in world; new restaurant every 14.5 hours*

The space on page 120 can be used for your rough answers.

Do not forget to put your answers on the back of Answer Sheet Two.

0   *McDonald's is a chain of fast-food restaurants which operates worldwide.*

81

82

83

84

85

86

87

88

PAPER 4   LISTENING   (APPROX. 45 MINUTES)

You will hear a talk about the wildlife found on golf courses. For questions 1–10, complete the sentences. You will hear the recording twice.

Wildlife on Golf Courses

New courses are being built on land previously used for

1 [_____].

Moles do damage to golf courses because they create

2 [_____] on the surface.

Another problem can be that a player's ball is removed from the hole by a

certain kind of **3** [_____].

When **4** [_____] are created on courses, wildlife quickly

appears there.

The variety of habitats on golf courses makes it easier for birds to

5 [_____].

The kind of **6** [_____] found on golf courses are not

dangerous for golfers and are useful because they eat creatures such as

7 [_____].

Wood ants are a danger on golf courses because

they **8** [_____] and **9** [_____].

It is said that **10** [_____] played an important part in the

invention of golf but they damage courses.

SECTION B

*You will hear the presenter of a radio programme about books giving details of a competition. For questions **11–17**, fill in the missing information.*

Listen very carefully because you will hear the recording only ONCE.

Writing Competition

Length of story: **11** [_____] *words*

Send entries and: **12** [_____]

Details to include: *Name, full address, and a number where you can be*

                      contacted **13** [_____]

Judges: *Magazine editor*

                      Novelist

                      14 [_____] *of TV plays*

First prize: *Story to be read on programme and*

                      15 [_____]

                      16 [_____] *, value £700*

Special prize for: **17** [_____]

SECTION C

You will hear part of a radio programme about making complaints. For questions 18–27, complete the sentences.
You will hear the piece twice.

MAKING COMPLAINTS

Both guests work for [18 _____] organizations.

If a company wants to have [19 _____], it will deal with

complaints quickly.

You should make complaints to someone with [20 _____].

If you do not make your complaint [21 _____], you may have

problems later.

Complaints about holidays should be made to a member of the travel company

[22 _____].

If you are given an unacceptable [23 _____] by a travel

company, you should consider going [24 _____] in order to get

[25 _____].

It is particularly difficult to get a complaint sorted out with [26 _____].

By law, the quality of goods bought in shops is the responsibility of

[27 _____].

SECTION D

You will hear extracts of five different people talking about buildings.
You will hear the series twice.

TASK ONE

*Letters **A–H** list buildings. As you listen, put them in the order in which you hear them being talked about by completing the boxes numbered **28–32** with the appropriate letter.*

A   a hotel

B   an arts centre

C   an airport

D   a shopping centre

E   a government building

F   a sports centre

G   an office block

H   a railway station

28	
29	
30	
31	
32	

TASK TWO

*Letters **A–H** list different opinions about the buildings expressed by the people speaking in the five extracts. As you listen, put them in the order in which you hear them by completing the boxes numbered **33–37** with the appropriate letter.*

A   you can easily get lost in it

B   it's bigger than necessary

C   there aren't enough facilities in it

D   it's attractive from the outside

E   it's difficult to find

F   there aren't enough places to sit down in it

G   it doesn't fit in with the surroundings

H   it is very similar to other buildings

33	
34	
35	
36	
37	

PAPER 5   SPEAKING   (15 MINUTES – 2 OR 3 CANDIDATES)

PHASE A (about 3 minutes)

Think of someone you know well, and introduce him/her by answering these questions:

> How did you get to know each other?
> Can you tell me something about his/her family?
> What does he/she do?
> What does he/she like doing in his/her spare time?
> What is his/her greatest ambition?

PHASE B (3 or 4 minutes)

1 Drawing Class (compare and contrast)

Candidate A should look at picture 5A on page 140
Candidate B should look at picture 5B on page 143

Your pictures are similar but not the same.

Candidate A should describe his/her picture in detail. You have about a minute to do this.

Candidate B should listen carefully. You should then talk about five things which are different in your picture and Candidate A's. If you need more help, you may ask Candidate A some questions.

After doing this you may compare your pictures.

2 At Home (describe and identify)

Candidate B should look at the pictures on page 141
Candidate A should look at the pictures on page 144

You each have the same pictures, but they are in a different order.

Candidate B should choose one of the pictures and describe it in detail. You should say something about the atmosphere of the picture and how you feel about it. You have about a minute to do this.

Candidate A should listen carefully. You should decide which picture Candidate B chose, and say how you knew this. If you need more help, you may ask Candidate B some questions.

After doing this you can compare both sets of pictures.

PHASE C (3 or 4 minutes)

Strangers (evaluation and rank ordering)

Both candidates should look at page 142, which shows the same set of pictures of eight different people. You have just arrived in a strange city, and have to ask for directions. These are the people you see around you in the street. Discuss which two of these people you would be **most likely** to stop and ask for directions, and which two you would be **least likely** to approach. Talk about each person and the reasons why you would approach him/her or not.

You and your partner may not agree. Be prepared to express his/her views as well as your own.

PHASE D (3 or 4 minutes)

How much do you think you judge other people on their appearance? Do you find this is a good guide to character? In which ways do you think people give information about themselves without speaking? Have you ever been badly mistaken about someone because you judged them too quickly on their appearance?

Do you think that what you wear to work can have an important effect on your career? What general advice about their appearance would you give to someone who is going to a job interview? Are there any particular jobs in which you think what people wear and look like really matters?

Have you ever tried to change your image by changing your appearance in some way? How successful were you? What would you most like to be able to change about your own appearance?

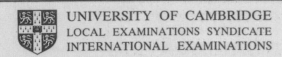

UNIVERSITY OF CAMBRIDGE
LOCAL EXAMINATIONS SYNDICATE
INTERNATIONAL EXAMINATIONS

ENGLISH AS A FOREIGN LANGUAGE

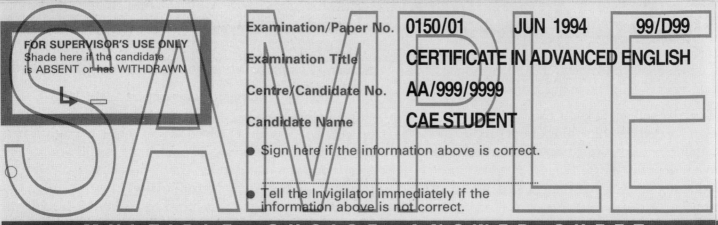

SAMPLE

Examination/Paper No.	**0150/01** **JUN 1994** **99/D99**
Examination Title	**CERTIFICATE IN ADVANCED ENGLISH**
Centre/Candidate No.	**AA/999/9999**
Candidate Name	**CAE STUDENT**

FOR SUPERVISOR'S USE ONLY
Shade here if the candidate
is ABSENT or has WITHDRAWN

- Sign here if the information above is correct.

....

- Tell the Invigilator immediately if the information above is not correct.

MULTIPLE—CHOICE ANSWER SHEET

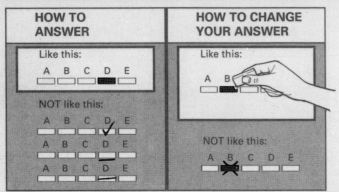

HOW TO ANSWER

Like this:

NOT like this:

HOW TO CHANGE YOUR ANSWER

Like this:

NOT like this:

DO
- use an HB pencil
- rub out any answer you wish to change

DON'T
- use any other kind of pen or pencil
- use correcting fluid
- make any marks outside the boxes

1	A B C D E F G H I J	21	A B C D E F G H I J	41	A B C D E F G H I J
2	A B C D E F G H I J	22	A B C D E F G H I J	42	A B C D E F G H I J
3	A B C D E F G H I J	23	A B C D E F G H I J	43	A B C D E F G H I J
4	A B C D E F G H I J	24	A B C D E F G H I J	44	A B C D E F G H I J
5	A B C D E F G H I J	25	A B C D E F G H I J	45	A B C D E F G H I J
6	A B C D E F G H I J	26	A B C D E F G H I J	46	A B C D E F G H I J
7	A B C D E F G H I J	27	A B C D E F G H I J	47	A B C D E F G H I J
8	A B C D E F G H I J	28	A B C D E F G H I J	48	A B C D E F G H I J
9	A B C D E F G H I J	29	A B C D E F G H I J	49	A B C D E F G H I J
10	A B C D E F G H I J	30	A B C D E F G H I J	50	A B C D E F G H I J
11	A B C D E F G H I J	31	A B C D E F G H I J	51	A B C D E F G H I J
12	A B C D E F G H I J	32	A B C D E F G H I J	52	A B C D E F G H I J
13	A B C D E F G H I J	33	A B C D E F G H I J	53	A B C D E F G H I J
14	A B C D E F G H I J	34	A B C D E F G H I J	54	A B C D E F G H I J
15	A B C D E F G H I J	35	A B C D E F G H I J	55	A B C D E F G H I J
16	A B C D E F G H I J	36	A B C D E F G H I J	56	A B C D E F G H I J
17	A B C D E F G H I J	37	A B C D E F G H I J	57	A B C D E F G H I J
18	A B C D E F G H I J	38	A B C D E F G H I J	58	A B C D E F G H I J
19	A B C D E F G H I J	39	A B C D E F G H I J	59	A B C D E F G H I J
20	A B C D E F G H I J	40	A B C D E F G H I J	60	A B C D E F G H I J

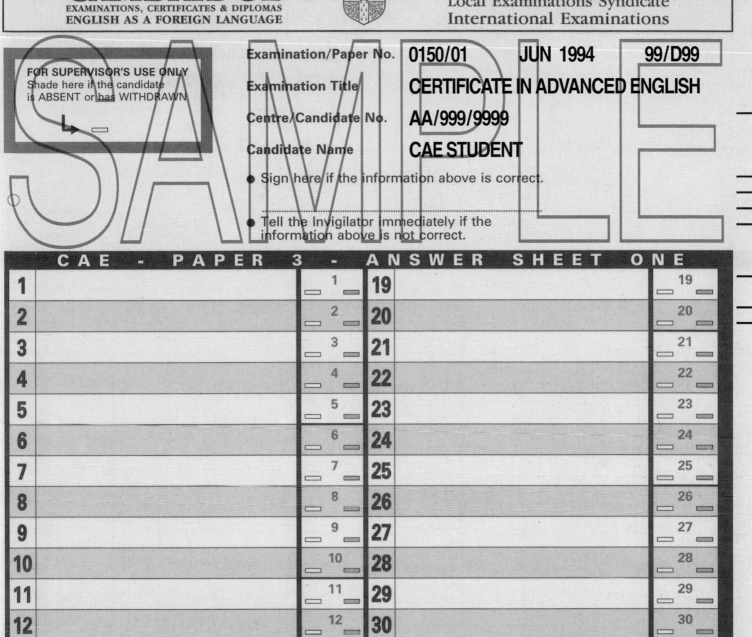

CAMBRIDGE

EXAMINATIONS, CERTIFICATES & DIPLOMAS
ENGLISH AS A FOREIGN LANGUAGE

University of Cambridge
Local Examinations Syndicate
International Examinations

FOR SUPERVISOR'S USE ONLY
Shade here if the candidate
is ABSENT or has WITHDRAWN

Examination/Paper No. **0150/01   JUN 1994   99/D99**

Examination Title **CERTIFICATE IN ADVANCED ENGLISH**

Centre/Candidate No. **AA/999/9999**

Candidate Name **CAE STUDENT**

● Sign here if the information above is correct.

....

● Tell the Invigilator immediately if the
information above is not correct.

CAE - PAPER 3 - ANSWER SHEET ONE

1	19
2	20
3	21
4	22
5	23
6	24
7	25
8	26
9	27
10	28
11	29
12	30
13	31
14	32
15	33
16	34
17	35
18	36

Continue on **ANSWER SHEET TWO** →

FOR OFFICE USE ONLY		
0 1 2	0 1 2	0 1 2
81	84	87
82	85	88
83	86	89

127

CAMBRIDGE
EXAMINATIONS, CERTIFICATES & DIPLOMAS
ENGLISH AS A FOREIGN LANGUAGE

University of Cambridge
Local Examinations Syndicate
International Examinations

FOR SUPERVISOR'S USE ONLY
Shade here if the candidate
is ABSENT or has WITHDRAWN

Examination/Paper No.	0150/01	JUN 1994	99/D99

Examination Title — **CERTIFICATE IN ADVANCED ENGLISH**

Centre/Candidate No. — **AA/999/9999**

Candidate Name — **CAE STUDENT**

● Sign here if the information above is correct.

....

● Tell the Invigilator immediately if the
information above is not correct.

CAE - PAPER 3 - ANSWER SHEET TWO

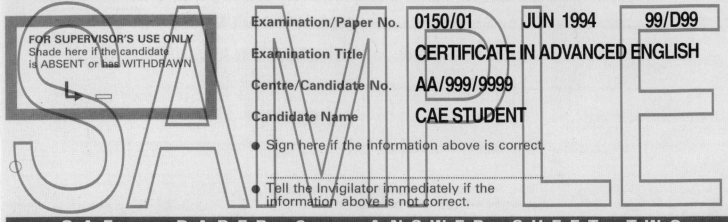

37		37	59		59
38		38	60		60
39		39	61		61
40		40	62		62
41		41	63		63
42		42	64		64
43		43	65		65
44		44	66		66
45		45	67		67
46		46	68		68
47		47	69		69
48		48	70		70
49		49	71		71
50		50	72		72
51		51	73		73
52		52	74		74
53		53	75		75
54		54	76		76
55		55	77		77
56		56	78		78
57		57	79		79
58		58	80		80

128

Continue on the OTHER SIDE of this sheet →

81

82

83

84

85

86

87

88

89

129

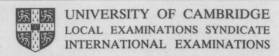

UNIVERSITY OF CAMBRIDGE
LOCAL EXAMINATIONS SYNDICATE
INTERNATIONAL EXAMINATIONS

ENGLISH AS A FOREIGN LANGUAGE

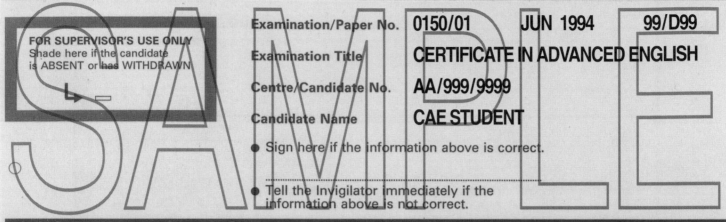

SAMPLE

Examination/Paper No.	**0150/01** **JUN 1994** **99/D99**
Examination Title	**CERTIFICATE IN ADVANCED ENGLISH**
Centre/Candidate No.	**AA/999/9999**
Candidate Name	**CAE STUDENT**

FOR SUPERVISOR'S USE ONLY
Shade here if the candidate
is ABSENT or has WITHDRAWN

● Sign here if the information above is correct.

....

● Tell the Invigilator immediately if the
information above is not correct.

LISTENING COMPREHENSION ANSWER SHEET

ENTER TEST NUMBER HERE →

FOR OFFICE USE ONLY →   [10][20][30][40][50]
[1][2][3][4][5][6][7][8][9]

1		1	21		21
2		2	22		22
3		3	23		23
4		4	24		24
5		5	25		25
6		6	26		26
7		7	27		27
8		8	28		28
9		9	29		29
10		10	30		30
11		11	31		31
12		12	32		32
13		13	33		33
14		14	34		34
15		15	35		35
16		16	36		36
17		17	37		37
18		18	38		38
19		19	39		39
20		20	40		40

1A

1B

1C

1D

1E

1F

1G

4A

2A

3A

3C

3D

1H

4B

2B

3B

3C

3D

1A

1B

1C

1D

1E

1F

2D

2F

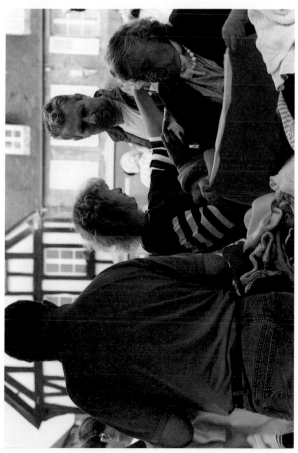

2C

2E

2G

2I

2H

2J

3E

4E

4C

5A

5C

5D

5E

5F

5G

5H

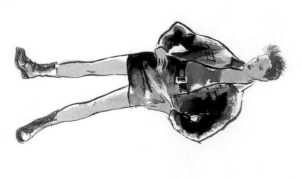

5M

5I

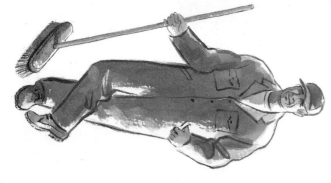

5N

5J

5O

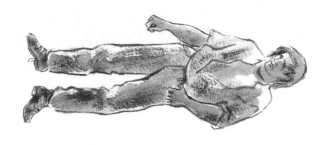

5K

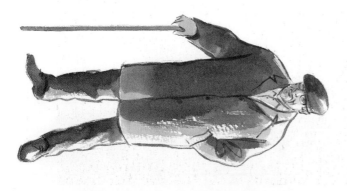

5P

5L

4D

5B

5C

5D

5E

5F

5G

5H

Note on marking: Each of the five papers in CAE contributes equally to the final grade. Raw scores for each paper are weighted to 40, giving a total weighted score of 200. The assessment criteria below and on page 146 are correct at time of publication, but may be subject to revision. See page 149 for the assessment criteria for Question 6, Paper 3.

Paper 2: Writing – Assessment criteria

The same assessment criteria are applied to both sections of the paper.

TASK-SPECIFIC assessment guidelines for each question will be added to the general criteria in order to define the type of organization, the register and the content required for each of the five questions.

NB:	Discrepancies between USE OF LANGUAGE and TASK ACHIEVEMENT require adjustment up or down on the impression scale.
5	Very positive effect on target reader. Minimal errors: resourceful, controlled and natural use of language showing good range of vocabulary and structure. Completion of task: well-organized, good use of cohesive devices, appropriate register, no relevant omissions. N.B. not necessarily a flawless performance!
4	Sufficiently natural, errors only when more complex language attempted. Some evidence of range of vocabulary and structure. Good attempt at task, only minor omissions. Attention paid to organization and cohesion; register not always natural but positive effect on target reader achieved.
3	Either a) task reasonably attempted, accuracy of language satisfactory but no notable variety, or b) an original attempt at the task, bringing in a range of vocabulary and structures which, however, cause a number of non-impeding errors, or c) a rather pedestrian approach to the task, possibly with some lifting (Section A) or rather limited range of structures/vocabulary but a good control of the fairly limited language used. No significant irrelevancies or omissions.
2	Errors sometimes obscure communication and/or language too elementary. Some attempt at task but notable omissions and/or lack of organization and cohesion would have negative effect on reader.
1	Serious lack of control and/or frequent basic errors. Narrow range of language. Inadequate attempt at task.
0	Either a) fewer that 50 words per question, b) totally illegible work, or c) total irrelevance.

Spelling: American spelling acceptable but there should be consistency. Poor spelling penalized by a one-band reduction if it interferes with communication.

Handwriting: Work which is difficult to read is penalized by a one or possibly two band reduction depending on degree of illegibility. Totally illegible work receives 0.

Length: Specific number of words used is not taken into account. Length is an integral part of task achievement. Significantly fewer words are likely to mean that the task has not been completed. Over-long pieces of writing may involve irrelevance or have a negative effect on the target reader and, only if this is the case, will be penalized.

Layout: Following the conventions of writing letters, reports and instructions is part of task achievement. Any acceptable modern layout for a formal letter may be used. Paragraphs should be indented although a space between each paragraph without indenting is a reasonable alternative.

Level 3 performance would indicate a pass at CAE level but the writer would probably need to make extensive checks on work, consult dictionaries and correct drafts.

Paper 5: Speaking – Assessment criteria

	Fluency	*Accuracy*	*Pronunciation*	*Task achievement*	*Interactive communication*
7–8	Coherent spoken interaction with good speed and rhythm. Few intrusive hesitations.	Evidence of a wide range of structures and vocabulary. Errors minimal in number and gravity.	Little L1 accent/L1 accent not obtrusive. Good mastery of English pronunciation features.	The tasks are dealt with fully and effectively. The language is appropriate to each task.	Contributes fully and effectively throughout the interaction.
5–6	Occasional but noticeable hestitations, but not such as to strain the listener or impede communication.	Evidence of a good range of structures and vocabulary. Errors few in number and minor in gravity. These errors do not impede communication.	Noticeable L1 accent having minor difficulties with some pronunciation features. These do not strain the listener or impede communication.	The tasks are mostly dealt with effectively but with minor inadequacies of execution of language.	Contributes with ease for most of the interaction, with only occasional and minor difficulties.
3–4	Fairly frequent and noticeable hesitations. Communication is achieved but strains the listener at times.	Fairly frequent errors and evidence of restricted range of structures and/or vocabulary. These do not prevent communication of the essential message.	Obvious L1 pronunciation features with major defects. These may strain the listener and/or make comprehension of detail difficult.	One or more of the tasks are dealt with in a limited manner. The language is often inappropriate. Redirection may have been required at times.	Contributes effectively for some of the interaction, but fairly frequent difficulties.
1–2	Disconnected speech and/or frequent hesitations impede communication and strain the listener.	Frequent basic errors and limited range of structures and/or vocabulary impede communication and strain the listener.	Heavy L1 pronunciation and widespread difficulties with English features impede communication of the message and strain the listener.	Inadequate attempts at the tasks using little appropriate language. Requires major redirection or assistance.	Difficulty in maintaining contributions throughout. May respond to simple or structured interaction but obvious limitations in freer situations.
0	Sample of language inadequate for assessment (even after prompting by the interlocutor).				

TEST 1
Paper 1

FIRST TEXT / This week's films on TV

1 / 2	A, D (any order)	12	E
3	D	13 / 14	D, I (any order)
4	C	15	A
5 / 6	A, G (any order)	16 / 17 /	
7 / 8	D, E (any order)	18	B, C, J (any order)
9	A	19	C
10 / 11	B, E (any order)		

SECOND TEXT / Justin has just the picture

20	E	24	G
21	B	25	C
22	F	26	H
23	A		

THIRD TEXT / Tips for air travellers

27	C	32 / 33	A, D (any order)
28	H	34	C
29	F	35	B
30	D	36	E
31	A	37 / 38	A, E (any order)

FOURTH TEXT / Art could take pain out of public transport

39	B	42	B
40	B	43	A
41	C	44	C

Paper 2

SECTION A

Question 1

There is a sample student answer on page 174.

Description of writing task:

CONTENT
Start the letter by explaining who you are and why you are writing. Include a description of how the holiday was spoilt, with clear reasons for your complaint. Should state that the publicity material is misleading, using evidence from the scientific report.

ORGANIZATION AND COHESION
Brief introduction. Clear paragraphing, with cohesive devices used to link the argument.

RANGE
Language to reflect personal experience; some use of scientific terms in relation to the report.

REGISTER
Formal; controlled indignation.

TARGET READER
Should take the letter seriously as a genuine complaint.

SECTION B

Question 2

Description of writing task:

CONTENT
Should include at least two 'attractions' and two trips or visits of a slightly off-beat nature.

ORGANIZATION AND COHESION
Trips etc. must not just be listed, but must be fully described so that it is clear why they are being recommended. Linguistic devices should show that one subject is finished and that the writer is moving on to the next one.

RANGE
Language needs to deal with description and recommendation. Vocabulary must be capable of conveying the attraction of the recommended place or activity.

REGISTER
Informal, with some approximation to popular journalistic style; light and colourful, with some eye-catching detail.

TARGET READER
Should feel really attracted by at least some of the ideas put forward.

Question 3

Description of writing task:

CONTENT
All questions should be answered, with information and instructions clearly given.

ORGANIZATION AND COHESION
Note should have friendly beginning and end. Content may be organized as partly on local travel, partly on longer trips. Alternative suggestions may be offered, linked by devices such as 'on the other hand'.

RANGE
Vocabulary needs to deal with transport and an idea of the sorts of areas (city, country, etc.) the visitor will be living in. Language of opinions and instructions will be used.

REGISTER
Informal but clearly informative.

TARGET READER
Should feel that s/he is receiving clear, reliable advice, given in a friendly way, not as orders or instructions or simply as information.

Question 4

Description of writing task:

CONTENT
Should include examples of good and bad features of the system. May be personal and anecdotal, but must also contain some analytical element.

ORGANIZATION AND COHESION
This could be a chronological account or experiences may be grouped together as good or bad, but in either case the point of mentioning any particular experience or feature of the system must be clear. A brief conclusion is needed at the end.

RANGE
Should cover opinion and exemplification, past tense narrative (what happened) and commentary on it/ conclusions drawn.

REGISTER
Personal experience is being quoted, but for unknown academic researchers, so a neutral, slightly formal style is needed.

TARGET READER
Should feel a thoughtful, reliable personal account is being given.

Question 5

Description of writing task:

CONTENT
The story line must be summed up briefly, so that comment and opinion are included, and the reason for recommendation to language learners must be plausible.

ORGANIZATION AND COHESION
As in a genuine review, a lot of information and opinion has to be packed into a small space, so the mode of expression needs to be to the point, with no padding.

RANGE
Must cover summary of events (present tense), recommendation and explanation.

REGISTER
Some approximation to a serious journalistic style, like a review from a quality paper.

TARGET READER
Should feel interested in seeing the film, play or musical, and should gain some impression of its qualities.

Paper 3

SECTION A

1 George Orwell

1	C	9	D
2	B	10	B
3	B	11	A
4	A	12	B
5	C	13	A
6	D	14	B
7	A	15	A
8	B		

2 Harry Houdini

16	down	24	could
17	himself	25	a
18	later/afterwards	26	which/that
19	allow/permit	27	all
20	so/and	28	the/his
21	nothing	29	belongs
22	except/but	30	like/want/wish
23	until/till		

SECTION B

3 The English Language

31	being	38	of
32	✓	39	✓
33	in	40	✓
34	which	41	one
35	so	42	of
36	✓	43	as
37	being	44	the

4 The Young Person's Railcard

45	value for	52	proof of
46	unlimited travel	53	education/study
47	entitles	54	application form
48	reductions	55	recommended
49	obtained	56	eligible
50	collected personally	57	have long
51	age limit/maximum age		

SECTION C

5 Aruba

Note:
There is no 'I' in this question and 'K' is always the example.

58	H	61	A
59	J	62	D
60	G	63	E

6 California

Note on marking:

Candidates are awarded an impression mark of 2, 1 or 0 for each of the items 81 to 88. The assessment criteria are as follows:

2 – acceptable response, linking the ideas successfully with only minor errors

1 – response successfully communicates the information required, but with major errors

0 – response communicates the wrong information and/or errors seriously impede intelligibility

Suggested answers:

81 Its nickname is the Golden State, originally because of its gold mines but more recently because of its sunshine.

82 Sacramento, which is the capital, Los Angeles and San Diego, which are both in the south, and San Francisco, which is in the north, are its main cities.

83 Physical features include Mount Whitney, which is the highest mountain in the USA excluding Alaska, and Death Valley, which is 96 metres below sea level.

84 It was a colony of Spain from 1769 to 1850, when it became a state of the US.

85 Gold was discovered there in January 1848 and this was followed by the 'gold rush' from 1849 to 1856.

86 It is the leading agricultural state and produces fruit, nuts and wheat, as well as many other products, including films and television programmes.

87 Since the 1950s many high-technology electronics firms have been based in Santa Clara county, which is known as 'Silicon Valley'.

88 Its population consists of 66% non-Hispanic white, 20% Hispanic, 7.5% black and 7% Asian, of whom many are Vietnamese.

Paper 4

SECTION A / Sick building syndrome

1	modern buildings
2	energy
3	out of/away from
4	personal
5	too hot
6	natural light
7	air conditioning
8	new materials
9	indoor air quality/quality of indoor air
10	maintenance
11	(building/furnishing) materials
12	(office) cleaning

SECTION B / Local sports centres

13	Sunday(s) evening(s)
14	Thursday(s) evening(s)
15	Saturday(s) all day/all day on Saturday(s)
16	volleyball
17	weekday lunchtimes/weekdays at lunchtime(s)/ (at) lunchtime on weekdays
18	weightlifting

SECTION C / Behaviour in crowds

19	Yes	25	No
20	No	26	No
21	Yes	27	No
22	No	28	Yes
23	Yes	29	No
24	Yes		

SECTION D / Different events

30	C	35	E
31	F	36	A
32	A	37	H
33	D	38	B
34	H	39	D

TEST 2
Paper 1

FIRST TEXT / Memories

1	C	4	A
2	B	5	C
3	A	6	D

SECOND TEXT / Get busy for a great break

7	E	17	D
8	D	18	E
9	H	19	A
10 / 11	G, J (any order)	20	J
12	A	21	G
13	F	22	D
14	G	23	C
15 / 16	B, I (any order)	24	F

THIRD TEXT / The animal dentist

25	F	29	E
26	G	30	A
27	D	31	I
28	B	32	C

FOURTH TEXT / Dreamland

33	E	38 / 39	B, C (any order)	
34	D	40	E	
35	F	41	A	
36	A	42	A	
37	A			

Paper 2

SECTION A

Question 1

There is a sample student answer on page 174.

Description of writing task:

CONTENT
Should include **all** the ideas and give reasons for liking or disliking them. Must identify the best entry (that is suitable for **all** children).

ORGANIZATION AND COHESION
Clear report format, demonstrating that the presentation of the ideas has been carefully planned. NB More than one possible way of presenting the different entries.

RANGE
Summarizing language; language of opinion.

REGISTER
Neutral report style, appropriate to a specialist publication.

TARGET READER
Should have a clear view of the winning entry and the other shortlisted ideas. Should be interested in the report.

SECTION B

Question 2

Description of writing task:

CONTENT
All questions should be answered in detail. May include any reasonable request for something to be brought from the USA.

ORGANIZATION AND COHESION
An appropriate beginning and ending to the letter are needed. Separate paragraphs for clothes/weather and for souvenirs, with some use of suitable linking phrases.

RANGE
Language must cover description, advice and possibly a polite request.

REGISTER
Friendly but polite and respectful.

TARGET READER
Should feel well informed and charmed.

Question 3

Description of writing task:

CONTENT
Should cover at least two aspects of social change in recent years, and commentary on this.

ORGANIZATION AND COHESION
Opinion could be linked to each change as it is mentioned, or a separate part of the article, but it must be clear what is being presented as fact and what as opinion.

RANGE
Description and commentary must both be present. Social trends may be described in semi-scientific terms. Anecdotes and personal experiences may be included, but should not replace impersonal reporting entirely.

REGISTER
Some approximation to the style of serious journalism. The subject is of general interest but should not be dealt with too lightly.

TARGET READER
Should receive clear information and opinions which are expressed with the emphasis on reason rather than emotion.

Question 4

Description of writing task:

CONTENT
This personal narrative must be credible, but out of the ordinary or amusingly presented enough to be eye-catching.

ORGANIZATION AND COHESION
This is probably an account of a series of events, so must have clear narrative progression. Ideally it should have varied pace and sound good when read aloud.

RANGE
There should be something in the vocabulary or presentation to lift it above the commonplace; this could be unusual events or humorous presentation.

REGISTER
Informal, conversational, amusing and anecdotal, but tightly controlled.

TARGET READER
Should be entertained.

Question 5

Description of writing task:

CONTENT
Must cover what the applicant has to offer, the place they want to work in and the reasons for applying.

ORGANIZATION AND COHESION
Letter format, with suitable formal beginning and end. Facts should be presented in a straghtforward way, and the letter clearly divided into the different aspects of the application.

RANGE
The description of skills and preferred workplace may be fairly impersonal, with a more personal note in the reasons for application. Some explanatory or persuasive language is needed, and use of the conditional (*if I were … I would …*) is likely.

REGISTER
Must deal with personal ambitions and experience, but in a fairly businesslike, impersonal way.

TARGET READER
Should feel a sensible, serious offer of useful skills is being made. Should wish to consider the applicant as a volunteer.

Paper 3

SECTION A

1 The Alexandra Palace

1	B	9	B
2	D	10	B
3	A	11	D
4	C	12	C
5	C	13	C
6	C	14	C
7	A	15	A
8	A		

2 New Horizons

16	from	24	which/that
17	in	25	chosen/selected/
18	becomes/gets		picked
19	having/needing/going	26	any
20	not	27	long
21	this	28	at
22	on	29	without
23	on	30	all/what

SECTION B

3 Freshwater fish

31	as	38	✓
32	it	39	to
33	✓	40	✓
34	✓	41	each
35	them	42	from
36	to	43	to
37	the	44	more

4 Book club complaint

45	inform you
46	dissatisfaction/anger/disappointment/annoyance/ displeasure
47	in writing/on paper
48	wrongly/incorrectly
49	supply me
50	In reply/In response
51	investigating/dealing with
52	contacted
53	to trace/to locate
54	correspondence
55	unhelpful/uncooperative
56	the terms/the conditions
57	not obliged
58	further payment(s)
59	resolved

SECTION C

5 Diving suits

60	D	63	H
61	F	64	G
62	B	65	A

6 Computer training

Suggested answers:
81 The college is situated in Atlanta House, a modern block with all modern facilities that is in the city centre and convenient for both buses and trains.
82 Hours are flexible to suit trainees and the college is open days, evenings and Saturdays.
83 It is the college's aim that trainees learn quickly and improve their skills in pleasant surroundings and a friendly atmosphere.
84 Courses are suitable for absolute beginners, those experienced with the latest systems and those who are seeking new career opportunities.
85 Classes are limited to a maximum of ten, individual attention is guaranteed and trainees can progress at their own pace.
86 All instructors are qualified and give guidance and encouragement at every stage.
87 Fees can be paid in full in advance with a twenty-five percent discount or in three monthly instalments.
88 The college Diploma is approved by most professional bodies and is guaranteed or fees are refunded.

Paper 4

SECTION A / Local attractions

1	castle
2	cathedral
3	castle ruins
4	transport museum
5	children half-price/half-price for children

6   cheap family ticket
7   boating lake
8   cheap family ticket
9   reductions for groups
10   rare breeds/Snake House
11   art gallery
12   theme park

SECTION B / Theatre information

13	comedy	18	(in) (the) balcony
14	credit card	19	thirty minutes
15	none	20	unemployed
16	ten or more	21	show/have/take/produce
17	3.00 p.m.		identification/identity

SECTION C / The translator

22	D	25	D
23	C	26	B
24	A	27	A

SECTION D / Our town

28	C	33	C
29	G	34	A
30	A	35	H
31	E	36	F
32	D	37	G

TEST 3
Paper 1

FIRST TEXT / The early years of the AA

1	C	10	J
2	H	11	D
3	B	12	F
4	D	13	E
5	A	14	E
6	I	15	J
7	A	16	B
8	C	17	A
9	H	18	A

SECOND TEXT / Actions speak louder than words

19	D	22	A
20	A	23	C
21	D	24	B

THIRD TEXT / 15 ways to lose a sale

25	K	31	M
26	I	32	D
27	N	33	G
28	A	34	A
29	O	35	F
30	L	36	C

FOURTH TEXT / Beethoven's piano

37	B	41	I
38	F	42	D
39	H	43	A
40	C	44	E

Paper 2

SECTION A

Question 1

There is a sample student answer on page 175.

Description of writing task:

CONTENT
a) Sympathetic response to Professor Pearce.
b) Invite Richard to stay; ask him to give a talk.

ORGANIZATION AND COHESION
a) Brief note
b) Suitably paragraphed letter, to cover both the invitation and the request.

RANGE
a) Original expressions to convey sympathy and understanding.
b) Friendly greetings; language of requests.

REGISTER
a) Formal; respectful tone.
b) Informal, enthusiastic and persuasive.

TARGET READER
a) Would be charmed.
b) Would be pleased to hear from an old friend and willing to help.

SECTION B

Question 2

Description of writing task:

CONTENT
Must cover all aspects of the topic given, and indicate low cost of each.

ORGANIZATION AND COHESION
As an entry in a handbook, this can be organized in sections under headings, or as a series of paragraphs.

RANGE
The language needs to deal with description, advice and possibility (*You might* …; *You could* …).

REGISTER
Informal written style.

TARGET READER
Should receive clear, basic information and feel that the writer understands the situation of a young traveller without much money.

Question 3

Description of writing task:

CONTENT
Should include a certain amount of factual information as well as opinions and aspirations.

ORGANIZATION AND COHESION
Report format – may use headings. Facts presented should be linked to conclusions drawn from them so that some coherent argument or standpoint is developed.

RANGE
Description of the present situation and expression of wishes/hopes for the future should both be present. There should be some language related to work and topics such as childcare – if the candidate has the expertise there could be some use of sociological vocabulary.

REGISTER
Serious, academic style is needed. Strong feelings may be expressed, but this must be done in a controlled way, backed by argument. Personal, anecdotal material may be used if it contributes to the argument.

TARGET READER
Should feel that s/he is learning something about another society, and should feel engaged with the topic.

Question 4

Description of writing task:

CONTENT
A good account of relevant experience and interests must be given, making clear both why you want to do the job and why you would be suitable for it.

ORGANIZATION AND COHESION
Letter format with appropriate beginning and end for job application. Clear links between experience and suitability must be made.

RANGE
Must cover personal qualities and past experiences and point out their relevance to this application. There will probably be some use of conditionals (*I could offer*…; *I would be able to*…).

REGISTER
Lively, but still formal enough for a job application.

TARGET READER
Should feel persuaded that the writer is energetic and fun, but also reliable and sensible. Should take the application seriously.

Question 5

Description of writing task:

CONTENT
Full details of a plausible situation – imaginary or based on a real case – must be given.

ORGANIZATION AND COHESION
There must be a clear progression from statement of the problem through the way of tackling it to the final achievement. A stong narrative thread should run through this piece of writing.

RANGE
Some vocabulary for describing environmental concerns will be necessary. Strong feelings may be expressed.

REGISTER
The style should not look out of place in a serious magazine, but this is also a personal account, and should be lively and enthusiastic.

TARGET READER
Should find the account of what the problem was and how it was overcome quite plausible, and should feel impressed by the achievement.

Paper 3

SECTION A

1 The motoring boom in the US

1	B	9	C
2	A	10	B
3	D	11	B
4	A	12	A
5	C	13	A
6	B	14	C
7	B	15	B
8	A		

2 Grapefruit

16	which	23	about/of/on
17	this	24	in
18	but/although/though	25	whether
		26	one
19	on	27	for/on
20	as	28	each
21	for	29	to
22	have	30	because/as/since/for

SECTION B

3 Mobile phones

31	completely	38	fitted
32	phones, most	39	separate
33	✓	40	✓
34	technology	41	high
35	portables, mobiles	42	continuous
36	✓	43	its
37	minutes'		

4 Competition for local musicians

44	go in	51	as long
45	Anyone can	52	last/take longer
46	your own	53	free use
47	form/put together/	54	appear/be on
	get together/start	55	come/are second
48	crowd	56	you want/like/choose/wish
49	judges	57	in touch/contact
50	written (ourselves)/	58	The/Her number
	made up/composed		
	(ourselves)		

SECTION C

5 Hay fever

59	F		62	E
60	G		63	D
61	A		64	J

6 The Wimbledon Lawn Tennis Championships

Suggested answers:
81 It is held at the All England Club in Wimbledon, which is a suburb in South-West London.
82 It lasts for a fortnight and takes place in the last week of June and the first week of July every year.
83 It started in 1877, when it was for men only and was won by Spencer Gore, who was British.
84 The club has eighteen courts, the biggest of which are Centre Court, where the finals are played, and Number One Court.
85 It was for amateurs only from 1877 to 1968, since when professionals have been allowed.
86 Martina Navratilova, who was the women's champion nine times, and Bjorn Borg, who was the men's champion five times, have been the winners of the championship the most times.
87 The last British men's champion was Fred Perry, who won it three times from 1934 to 1936 and the last British women's champion was Virginia Wade, who won it in 1977.
88 It is one of the four main tournaments, the others being the Australian, the French and the US Opens, which together form the Grand Slam.

Paper 4

SECTION A / Malawi

1	in the 1960s
2	long as
3	no harbours
4	(the ship's) lifeboats
5	people and mail/goods/supplies
6	the western side
7 / 8	electricity/water (in any order)
9	home-made
10	unique species/kinds/types/sorts of fish
11	in the 1950s
12	pollution

SECTION B / Animal watch

13	an animal park
14	money
15	illegal hunting/hunters
16	Explorers News
17	discounts
18	by/on the/if you phone

SECTION C / Children's book writers

19	Yes	24	No
20	No	25	Yes
21	No	26	No
22	Yes	27	Yes
23	No	28	No

SECTION D / Recent purchases

29	D	34	A
30	G	35	D
31	C	36	G
32	A	37	F
33	E	38	E

TEST 4
Paper 1

FIRST TEXT / Doodles

1	A	10	J
2	B	11	A
3	J	12	B
4	H	13	C
5	E	14	J
6	E	15	G
7	H	16	I
8	G	17	D
9	C	18	D

SECOND TEXT / The organic farm

19	B	23	A
20	C	24	B
21	D	25	C
22	A		

THIRD TEXT / Up, up in the air

26	D	30	B
27	C	31	H
28	F	32	A
29	G		

FOURTH TEXT / Beliefs about bees

33	D	39	E
34	B	40	C
35	G	41	J
36	I	42	I
37	F	43	H
38	I	44	A

Paper 2

SECTION A

Question 1

There is a student sample answer on page 175.

Description of writing task:

CONTENT
Introductory reference to Gerald Bell's letter. Clear explanation of why you are writing. Some description of the visit, with strong reasons why it is beneficial.

ORGANIZATION AND COHESION
Good use of cohesive devices to strengthen the argument.

RANGE
Descriptive language of past events; giving opinions and recommendations.

REGISTER
Formal letter; forceful but controlled.

TARGET READER
Would be convinced that the person knows what they are talking about and would publish the letter.

Section B

Question 2

Description of writing task:

CONTENT
Both questions must be addressed. Anecdotes and personal examples and opinions are appropriate, as long as it is clear that they are being put forward as such, and not as accepted fact. The impression given should be positive and encouraging to the original writer.

ORGANIZATION AND COHESION
Letter format is not important here, as what is being written is more like a newspaper article than a true letter.

RANGE
Candidates with any special interest in the subject could argue from academic knowledge, but most should be relating opinions based on personal (and friends') experiences.

REGISTER
Lively and informal, friendly and encouraging.

TARGET READER
Should be interested, reassured, possibly surprised by the arguments put forward.

Question 3

Description of writing task:

CONTENT
The candidate need not work through all the issues mentioned, but will probably cover at least two or three, and mention at least one or two areas where change is needed.

ORGANIZATION AND COHESION
Could be set out as a report, with short paragraphs under subheadings, but anyone who does this should be careful to develop some points fully, and not just produce a series of one-sentence paragraphs.

RANGE
Straightforward present tense description is needed, with a wide vocabulary for describing work conditions, social benefits, etc. Use of conditional for mentioning things which could be better.

REGISTER
Impersonal and businesslike report.

TARGET READER
Should feel s/he has learned a lot about the subject.

Question 4

Description of writing task:

CONTENT
Must cover two topics equally fully.

ORGANIZATION AND COHESION
The article must be clearly divided into two sections, each probably under a subheading, and with its own appropriate opening and closing sentences.

RANGE
A wide range of vocabulary is needed, but fairly simple present tense structures.

REGISTER
Should be suitable for a popular publication: informative but also lively and informal.

TARGET READER
Should be above all informed, but may also be entertained.

Question 5

Description of writing task:

CONTENT
Must include details of what was wrong with accommodation, travelling distance and family, but should mention some good aspects of the experience too.

ORGANIZATION AND COHESION
Letter format, with suitable opening and closing sentences. The case for complaining must be carefully developed.

RANGE
Language needs to handle backing up complaints with reasons for them. The connections should be clear.

REGISTER
The complaints should be politely expressed, in a formal and controlled manner.

TARGET READER
Should feel the writer has a good case for complaint and is being reasonable in his/her reaction to a difficult situation.

Paper 3

SECTION A

1 How we read

1	C	9	A
2	A	10	A
3	A	11	B
4	C	12	A
5	B	13	D
6	A	14	A
7	D	15	B
8	C		

2 Trees

16	have	24	they
17	much	25	which
18	of	26	to
19	them	27	is
20	to	28	the
21	it	29	over/above
22	there	30	even
23	more		

SECTION B

3 Midsummer in Finland

31	✓	38	✓
32	as	39	✓
33	the	40	one
34	the	41	make
35	a	42	themselves
36	to	43	✓
37	so	44	as

4 Terms of employment

45	have to/need to	52	serve/deal with
46	on time	53	quickly/fast
47	regularly/frequently/ often late	54	polite to/friendly to/ pleasant to/nice to
48	the sack/sacked/ fired	55	ask someone
49	smart/smartly dressed/ dressed smartly	56	ready before
		57	making sure/ checking
50	be allowed	58	always full
51	try hard	59	pay me

SECTION C

5 Card game rules

60	E	63	C
61	J	64	G
62	B	65	H

6 Concorde

Suggested answers:
81 It was developed in the 1950s as a result of cooperation between Britain and France and has a distinctive bird-like shape.
82 Its first flight was in March, 1969 and it became the first supersonic airliner in commercial service in January, 1976.
83 It is 70 metres long, has a wing span of 29 metres and can carry a maximum of 100 passengers.
84 It flies at twice the speed of sound, which it first achieved in 1970.
85 It is operated by British Airways and Air France and flies to various destinations, including from London to New York and Miami and from Paris to New York.
86 It also makes special flights, such as trips to Lapland during the Christmas period, trips to Cairo, Moscow and Vienna and day trips from London to Paris.
87 The average flight time from London to New York is 3 hours and 40 minutes although the record, which was set in April, 1990, is 2 hours, 55 minutes.
88 For passengers there are seats made of soft leather, one member of the crew for each 16 passengers, a five-course meal, and a free gift.

Paper 4

SECTION A / The ring-pull can

1	economical/cheap	7	too shallow
2	leak(s)	8	too deep
3	0.28 millimetres/mm	9	V-shape
4	0.09 millimetres/mm	10	square
5	cleanly and easily	11	to release pressure
6	reliable	12	just over a/one penny

SECTION B / What's on this weekend

13	No	17	No
14	Yes	18	No
15	Yes	19	Yes
16	No	20	No

SECTION C / The explorer

21	failed/been failures	27	without (having) enough food/
22	no deaths		without eating enough
23	the planning	28	the physical challenge
24/25	the equipment/ the training (in any order)	29	the South Pole
		30	more food
26	disease research centre		

SECTION D / Talking about other people

31	D	36	G
32	A	37	C
33	F	38	A
34	G	39	F
35	E	40	D

TEST 5

Paper 1

FIRST TEXT / Big Bill Broonzy

1	F	5	E
2	B	6	A
3	C	7	H
4	I	8	G

SECOND TEXT / Household goods

9	C	17	G
10	A	18	G
11/12	C, D (any order)	19	C
13	F		
14/ 15/16	A, E, G (any order)		

THIRD TEXT / Code of practice

20	C	30	G
21	D	31/32	J, K (any order)
22	I	33	D
23/24	H, J (in any order)	34	F
25	F	35	B
26	M	36	H
27	L	37	E
28	B		
29	L		

FOURTH TEXT / Voluntary Service Overseas

38	C	41	D
39	C	42	A
40	D	43	C

Paper 2

SECTION A

Question 1

There is a student sample answer on page 176.

Description of writing task:

CONTENT
a) Should cover future plans, with a tactful refusal of Mrs Milne's offer.
b) Request several items of information.

ORGANIZATION AND COHESION
a) Appropriate opening and concluding sentence; clear paragraphing.
b) Brief, clear set of enquiries.

RANGE
a) Suitable expressions of tact; use of polite forms.
b) Some specialist vocabulary related to courses.

REGISTER
a) Respectful but friendly.
b) Neutral, semi-formal.

TARGET READER
a) Would not feel offended at the refusal.
b) Would know exactly how to respond.

SECTION B

Question 2

Description of writing task:

CONTENT
Should be equally divided between explanation and advice. Will probably concentrate on social customs, public behaviour, clothes, religion, attitudes to women, children, etc.

ORGANIZATION AND COHESION

The opening paragraph should detail the sorts of problems which arise, and there should be some sort of reassurance at the end.

RANGE

There should be a good range of tactful ways of suggesting, explaining and advising.

REGISTER

There should be some evidence that the writer realizes that this is a delicate subject, needing tact and subtlety in its handling. The writing should not have an alienating or patronizing effect.

TARGET READER

Should feel informed without being made to feel awkward or offended.

Question 3

Description of writing task:

CONTENT

As well as the details mentioned, advice/information may cover what clothes and domestic or sports equipment to bring, and general information on study and social facilities in the school, college or workplace.

ORGANIZATION AND COHESION

Letter format, with friendly introduction and ending.

RANGE

Language covers description and advice.

REGISTER

Friendly, but not over-familiar.

TARGET READER

Should feel in contact with someone who is pleased to be helpful, but is keeping a respectful distance.

Question 4

Description of writing task:

CONTENT

Should include a description of the existing range of TV channels and what they have to offer, and then go on to assess what is good and what needs to be changed.

ORGANIZATION AND COHESION

Report format. Subheadings may be used to divide the material, but the candidate should be careful not to produce a series of one-sentence paragraphs.

RANGE

The vocabulary used has to be able to handle terms for different types of programmes and for assessing their qualities. Structures need to cover description of the present situation and wishes/hopes for future change.

REGISTER

Objectively presented, yet involving strong personal opinions.

TARGET READER

Should feel reliably informed, whether or not s/he has the same tastes in TV programmes.

Question 5

Description of writing task:

CONTENT

The candidate must go well beyond a simple re-telling of the story/subject of the book, and include reasons for liking it, and the sorts of people it will be useful to.

ORGANIZATION AND COHESION

There must be at least three paragraphs, to cover each of the listed points, and a clear progression from one point to the next.

RANGE

The ability to write a brief summary of a book must be clear, and to express the reason for liking it, and justify the recommendation that the library should buy it.

REGISTER

Personal opinions expressed in a fairly formal way.

TARGET READER

Should feel that the book would be a good investment for the library.

Paper 3

SECTION A

1 The body clock

1	D	9	D
2	A	10	C
3	A	11	B
4	B	12	B
5	D	13	A
6	C	14	C
7	A	15	A
8	A		

2 Chess tournaments

16	which/that	24	has
17	Whoever	25	to
18	matter	26	what
19	up	27	on
20	in	28	without
21	is	29	the
22	a/any	30	have
23	down/up		

SECTION B

3 American Indians

31	thirty-year	38	✓
32	violence	39	opportunity
33	✓	40	varied
34	tales	41	willingness
35	occasionally	42	interpreter's
36	lost, those	43	Indian's
37	✓		

4 College film society

44	set up/established/founded
45	appointed (as)/elected (as)/chosen as
46	demand for/desire for/interest in
47	response to/view of/line with
48	firm/fixed/set views/opinions
49	nature of/titles of
50	welcome/appreciate
51	intended/planned/projected/envisaged
52	weekly basis
53	no charge
54	membership
55	cover/meet the
56	refreshments
57	available/provided/served/sold
58	Anyone/Those wishing/wanting

SECTION C

5 Film company trademarks

59	G	62	A
60	H	63	E
61	F	64	D

6 McDonald's

Suggested answers:

81 It was founded by Ray Kroc, who got the idea from a small stall in California called McDonald's Hamburgers, which was run by two brothers, Mac and Dick McDonald.

82 The first restaurant was an outdoor one in Chicago, which opened in 1955 and sold hamburgers, fries and milk shakes.

83 In 1963, the 500th/five hundredth restaurant opened, new products were introduced and income was over one million dollars/$1m.

84 In 1967 the first indoor restaurants and the first restaurants outside the US opened and the first nationwide television advertisements were shown in the US.

85 In 1971 restaurants opened in Japan, Australia, Germany and other countries and there was a McDonald's in every state in the US.

86 Breakfast food started in 1977 and later McDonald's served twenty-five percent/a quarter/25% of all breakfasts eaten outside the home in the US.

87 In 1984 there were eighteen/18 million customers per day, which is equivalent to lunch for the entire population of Australia and New Zealand.

88 In 1990 more than a hundred/100 hamburgers every second were sold throughout the world and a new restaurant opened every fourteen and a half/14.5 seconds.

Paper 4

SECTION A / Wildlife on golf courses

1	farming/agriculture	6	snakes
2	piles of earth	7	mice
3	bird	8 / 9	bite/sting (in any order)
4	ponds and lakes	10	rabbits
5	find food		

SECTION B / Writing competition

11	(a) maximum of/maximum/up to/no more than/less than 2,500
12	(a) postcard
13	during/in the daytime/day
14	(a) writer
15	published in Your World (magazine)
16	(a) word processor
17	(the) most original/most unusual story/entry

SECTION C / Making complaints

18	consumer(s/s')
19	a good reputation/good public relations
20	authority
21	quickly/immediately/promptly
22	on the spot
23	excuse
24	to court
25	compensation
26	some large companies
27	the shop/shops/the shop itself/shops themselves

SECTION D / Buildings

28	G	33	A
29	B	34	C
30	D	35	G
31	A	36	D
32	C	37	E

TAPESCRIPTS

TEST 1

*There are four sections to this test – A, B, C and D. You will hear Section B **once** only. All the other parts of the test will be heard twice.*

During the test, there will be a pause before each part to allow you to look through the questions, and other pauses to let you think about your answers. At the end of every pause you will hear this sound. FX

You should write your answers on the question paper. You will have ten minutes at the end to transfer your answers to the separate answer sheet.

The tape will now be stopped. You must ask any questions now, as you will not be allowed to speak during the test. PAUSE 00'10"

SECTION A   Sick Building Syndrome

You will hear a talk about Sick Building Syndrome, which is ill health that is believed to be caused by buildings. For questions 1–12, complete the sentences.

You will hear the recording twice.

Have you ever gone back to work after a break or a holiday and been suddenly hit by a complete lack of energy? And you wonder whether it's simply because you're not relaxing any more but you think that perhaps it's something else, something to do with your environment. Well, you could be right. In 1982, the World Health Organization defined Sick Building Syndrome as "a syndrome of complaints covering non-specific feelings of ill health, the onset of which is associated with the occupancy of certain modern buildings". To those suffering from it, it means feelings of lack of energy, headaches, dry skin, even itchy eyes. And while the general view might be that there's a chance of getting sick if you work in a factory and that you wouldn't expect to feel unwell when you go to work in offices, this is not true. The office, it seems, is not the safe and healthy environment it is traditionally thought to be.

Surveys among office workers have revealed that large numbers of them in the same building can be affected by the symptoms. Some are affected only from time to time, and others all week but a common finding was that sufferers were mainly affected at the beginning of the week and when they'd been out of the building for some time. And the symptoms disappeared quite quickly when they left work. However, the problem is often a hidden one because many people don't associate the problems with their environment, they think it's probably something about them themselves. And they often say nothing about it because if they do so they might be accused of being complainers. It has been suggested that the problems could arise for reasons as simple as that the central heating is too high. But it is a mistake to look for simple explanations of what is a complex matter. It *could* be just that the heating is up too high but this does not explain the range of symptoms that sufferers in the same building can have or the fact that these occur in buildings with similar

characteristics. It is not possible to generalize about which features of a building cause the problems. A lack of windows that open and of natural light may well play a part but there is no proof that these are the main causes. However, there are certain types of building that are more prone to Sick Building Syndrome than others. Air-conditioned buildings are more likely to produce the symptoms than naturally ventilated ones and buildings that have large amounts of new materials, for example plastics and new carpets, are more likely to produce them too. Experts now think that the most important aspect is the indoor air quality, what kind of air you are breathing, what kind of air is in contact with your skin. There's a range of pollutants in buildings, from dust to carbon dioxide to the very many organic compounds which can become gases and be released from office materials and furnishings.

These, therefore, are the two aspects that experts are looking at in an attempt to address the problem. There is no reason why air-conditioning systems shouldn't be operated in a safe and healthy way but the fact is that they are often not sufficiently well-maintained and sometimes that's because they haven't been designed with this in mind. And with regard to the building and furnishing materials that are used to put a building together, there are now a range of materials on the market which produce less pollution.

There's one other aspect, too. In older buildings, research has shown that one of the big problems is office cleaning. Experiments have been done where offices have been cleaned and the symptoms of sufferers have been reduced almost overnight by up to 40%.

So, although the problem is not going to go away quickly, there are now the means to address the problem and more knowledge of it than there was when the World Health Organization first started looking into it.

SECTION B   Local Sports Centres
You will hear part of a local radio programme in which details about sports facilities in the area are given. For questions 13–18, fill in the missing details.

Listen very carefully because you will hear the recording only once.

Next we come to sports facilities and as you may know we have three excellent sports centres in our area. So if you feel like taking up a sport, improving your abilities at one or joining in with others to play, there's no shortage of opportunities for you. Between them, our three centres cover just about every sport you could mention. First of all, the Springfield Centre. Opened only a year ago, it has a swimming pool complex, conference facilities, an athletics track and an outdoor area with football and hockey pitches. The swimming pool complex caters for casual swimming and diving and there are also lessons and competitions. Swimming lessons and coaching are available on Saturday and Sunday evenings, with diving courses on the latter. The athletics track attracts top athletes, clubs and schools. Coaching for this – both running and field events – is on Thursday evenings, when there are also football coaching sessions, and if you want to improve your hockey, Wednesday evenings are for you. By the way, non-sporting events such as holiday activities and firework displays are also held at the Centre. Numerous sports are on offer at the Postbridge Centre too. There are ten indoor tennis courts there, and the

Saturday coaching sessions have proved so popular that they've been extended from mornings only and are now available all day. Aspiring footballers can enrol for coaching sessions there too – they're on Fridays and Saturdays, all day – and if you fancy joining a volleyball or a basketball team you can do that too. Coaching for the former is on Wednesday evenings and for the latter on Thursday evenings and Sunday afternoons. Finally there's the Avenue Centre, which again caters for a wide variety of sports. You can improve your backhand there too – there are tennis lessons every weekday at lunchtimes and badminton and table tennis tuition, in both cases on Friday evenings. If weightlifting is your thing, then this is the place for you, with coaching offered on Saturday mornings. And there's gymnastics too, with highly qualified instructors taking training sessions on Tuesday evenings. So, there's no excuse for being lazy in this area! If you want more details on any of the things I've mentioned, get in touch with the centres themselves. They'll be pleased to hear from you.

SECTION C   Behaviour in Crowds
You will hear part of a radio programme, in which a psychologist talks about the way people behave in crowds and groups. For questions 19–29, indicate which views he expresses by writing Yes or No in the box provided.

You will hear the piece twice.

Presenter: ... I'm joined on the line now by social psychologist David Macintosh. David, is it natural for our behaviour to change when we're in a crowd environment?
Psychologist: Well ... yes ... it's natural in the sense that people typically do that. I mean, one very simple example is that you very rarely laugh by yourself but when you're in a crowd of people, say at some funny film, play or whatever ... um ... it's very common to find yourself laughing out loud.
Presenter: So what sorts of behaviour do you find in a crowd environment, then?
Psychologist: A number of things. I mean, what generally one can say is that people have needs to be with people for various reasons – family, friends, activities – and they also, um, get things out of simply being in a larger crowd. Sometimes it's just a sense of being, er, somewhat more anonymous. They sometimes also get an amplification of feelings. I mean, for example at concerts ... er ... in football crowds, feelings seem to get heightened and sometimes there's something really nice about getting a strong sense of being part of a large group.
Presenter: Why should we become disruptive in some sorts of crowd environments, then, why should there sometimes be that element of aggression?
Psychologist: A couple of possibilities. One is the

thing that crowds very often seem to amplify feelings and so they can amplify bad as well as good feelings. Um, the other is ... what's often been suggested is, that we have a number of kinds of identities. I mean, one, which is the predominant one, is our everyday one but there are others and what happens in crowds is that we can sometimes shift, if you like, our identity and what a crowd picks up on are other aspects of ourselves, which might sometimes be the less pleasant ones, the more destructive ones.
Presenter: Now if we focus on the animal kingdom, does the same thing happen there?
Psychologist: Um, you get something like that. What you get with some animals of course, is that you get examples of very coordinated groups, like small fish schooling so that they look like a large fish to possible predators and ... um ... you get, you know, lions hunting in packs and um ... you get large groups of animals like ... um ... ants and bees and so on who act in a very highly structured way, which is much less typical of humans except in odd circumstances like armies. But they sometimes also have disruptive tendencies – you get packs of animals scattering in panic too.
Presenter: So this feeling of amplification when we're in a crowd can lead us to act in an uncharacteristic way then, from what you're saying?

Psychologist: Uncharacteristic in the sense that it's what we don't normally do but it's not, as it were, not *ours*. The behaviour is there, only it's usually kept under control.

Presenter: Now the *group* situation, rather than the crowd, that's very different again, isn't it?

Psychologist: It is rather. I mean, in a group you're focused *in*, you're looking inwards, you're not worried about people outside. What's very clear is there's a very strong sense of being a member of a group, of a very defined little set, it's us versus them.

Presenter: And it gives you a sense of security presumably?

Psychologist: It does. It's familiar, it's comfortable and it also reinforces, if you like, your sense of yourself because you're very aware of yourself as a member of that group, as being a person among friends. And that also helps you relax in various ways, you're comfortable about your behaviour, you're defined as a friend among friends and therefore you don't have to worry about how you appear so much.

Presenter: Does your behaviour still change slightly? You've talked about a crowd's effect on an individual, surely still a small group will change you in some way sometimes?

Psychologist: Oh that's true. As I've said, we have a number of identities and our identity varies depending on the kind of group we're in. In a particular group we have a particular kind of identity with certain behaviour, so that when you're with a group of friends you relax, laugh, play the fool, but there are other groups you're members of where you behave differently, groups of workmates for example, um … more formal groups. And so in a sense you have different roles depending on what group you happen to be in at a given time. I think most of us are aware that this happens, that we are different kinds of people in different kinds of situations.

Presenter: David Macintosh, thanks very much for talking to us.

SECTION D   Different events

You will hear extracts of five different people talking about events.   You will hear the series twice.

TASK ONE Letters A–H list different events. As you listen, put them in the order in which you hear them described by completing the boxes numbered 30–34 with the appropriate letter.

TASK TWO Letters A–H list what the people in the five extracts are doing when they are speaking. As you listen, put them in the order in which you hear them by completing the boxes numbered 35–39 with the appropriate letter.

Voice 1: You ought to go to one some time, you'd probably enjoy it. I mean, even if you don't know what's going on out there on the pitch, you'll be impressed by the atmosphere – the noise of the crowd, the singing, the chanting and all that. I know there's a lot of talk about how much trouble goes on at some of them but you don't find that sort of thing round here, it's all just people cheering on their side – some of them get really worked-up but it's always well-behaved. I'd certainly give it a try if I were you.

Voice 2: Quite frankly, the whole thing was appalling. It cost a fortune to get in and from where I was you could hardly see anything. In the interval I had to queue for ages to get an overpriced drink and I missed some of the rest of it because of that. Not that it made much difference, because I couldn't really follow the plot anyway – I couldn't tell who was who or what was going on. No wonder audiences are falling these days. If that's the kind of thing they put on and if that's the way you get treated, there must be lots of people who get fed up and don't bother going again.

Voice 3: What's the point in turning up for something like that? I'll tell you what the point is. You ought to stand up and be counted. I mean, if everyone thought like you, nothing would ever get done and even if we don't win, we should all state our case, it's the least we can do. Everyone in this community is threatened by what they're planning and that includes you, so don't be so apathetic. I mean, if you just sit back and take it now because you can't be bothered to go and join in the march this afternoon, you can hardly complain afterwards, when it's too late.

Voice 4: Since you ask, I'll tell you. The last one was a complete and utter waste of time. I mean, you were there, you saw it. It was total chaos, with everybody yelling and shouting, no sort of organization at all and just a lot of people being totally unreasonable. And what was the outcome? Not a single thing got sorted out or decision made. So you can hardly be surprised that I've had enough. I mean, that really is it as far as I'm concerned. You can all get on with it without me from now on. It's no good trying to talk me into it. I've resigned and I won't be turning up again.

Voice 5: I suppose you've got a point actually, it was a bit crowded there, which did make it a bit uncomfortable – I guess they asked too many people for the size of the place – but in all honesty it didn't particularly bother me. And now you mention it, they hadn't really laid on enough for such a big crowd to eat – it did run out fairly early but I'd had enough by then. Oh and you're right about some of those people they'd invited acting very strangely – I wonder who they were – but they certainly stopped the thing from becoming a bore. I'm with you about the horrid music as well but I have to say, I've certainly been to worse.

That is the end of Section D. There will now be a ten minute pause to allow you to transfer your answers to the separate answer sheet. Be sure to follow the numbering of all the questions. The question papers and answer sheets will then be collected by your supervisor.

TEST 2

*There are four sections to this test – A, B, C and D. You will hear Section B **once** only. All the other parts of the test will be heard twice.*

During the test, there will be a pause before each part to allow you to look through the questions, and other pauses to let you think about your answers. At the end of every pause you will hear this sound. FX

You should write your answers on the question paper. You will have ten minutes at the end to transfer your answers to the separate answer sheet.

The tape will now be stopped. You must ask any questions now, as you will not be allowed to speak during the test. PAUSE 00'10"

SECTION A   Local Attractions
You will hear part of a radio programme, in which the presenter is talking about the attractions of an area. For questions 1–12, make a note of the attractions and what is offered at them.
You will hear the recording twice.

Presenter: … and now we come to our regular ''Have a Break'' feature. Today we're looking at the northern region of the country and what it has to offer if you visit it or if you live there and fancy a day out.

Well, perhaps the best-known town is Halford. While it has a host of fascinating old buildings, its main attraction is of course the castle, which is over 800 years old and widely considered to be the best-preserved in the country. It is a splendid building, set in lovely grounds, and there are reduced admission charges for groups.

If you want to see one of the finest cathedrals in the country, Linbury is the place to visit. Guided tours are available there, on which you can learn all about the fascinating history of the place, but if you prefer to just wander around this magnificent building on your own, or attend a service, you can do so.

Another place offering guided tours is Lewiston, where the castle ruins are well worth a visit. These, too, have a fascinating history, and you can hear all about the battles that took place there hundreds of years ago.

Children and parents alike will thoroughly enjoy the Transport Museum in Rockfield. There, you can see some of the oldest cars, bikes and buses in the world – some of them look quite incredible to us today! Children get in for half-price, so it's not only a good day out for all the family, but an inexpensive one, too.

Another place that gives good value for money for families is the zoo at Buckton. The cheap family ticket offered there gives you the chance to take the kids to see the elephants and all the rest without spending a fortune.

You can also get a cheap family ticket at the boating lake in Westhill. It covers an enormous area and is in very picturesque countryside, so if you fancy a pleasant, lazy afternoon on the water, this is the place for you.

If you've never been to the castle at Slone, it's well worth a visit. Although smaller than the one at Halford, it's very impressive and, as there, groups get in cheaper. It's easy to find, too – it's perched on top of a hill above the town and you can't miss it.

There are special group rates at Loxton Zoo, also. It's not as big as the one at Buckton, but it has some rare breeds, and its Snake House is particularly popular.

If Art is to your taste, the place for you is Coundon, whose gallery has a worldwide reputation. If you wish, you can take guided tours there, where art experts and historians will draw your attention to some of the more interesting and famous exhibits and give you information that will help you to appreciate what you see.

Finally, the theme park at Trace is particularly good value for families. Children are half-price and there is lots for them to do there, including some of the most exciting rides to be found anywhere.

If you would like our information sheet on all these places, please send a stamped addressed envelope to …

SECTION B   Theatre Information
You will hear a theatre's recorded information service. For questions 13–21, make a note of the information given.

Listen very carefully because you will hear the recording only once.

This is the York Theatre recorded information service, with details of our current production, the comedy *The Dream*.

Tickets can be obtained in person from the Box Office, which is open from 10 a.m. to 8 p.m. Monday to Saturday and on Sunday from 12 noon to 4 p.m. For credit card bookings, call 071-379 4454. There is no booking fee for this service.

Group bookings can be made for all performances on weekdays by phoning 071-947 9875 between 9.30 a.m. and 5.30 p.m. Monday to Friday. There are reduced rates for groups of 10 or more.

Performance times are as follows: Tuesday to Friday 7.45; Saturday 3.00 p.m. and 7.45; Sunday 3.00 p.m.

Please note that there is no performance on Mondays and that the only performance on Sunday is the matinee performance at 3.00 p.m.

Ticket prices: £14.00, £16.50 and £18.50 in the stalls; £9.00, £12.00 and £16.50 in the circle. In the balcony, all seats are £5.00. In addition, boxes are available at £16.50 per seat.

A certain number of standby tickets may be available 30 minutes before the performance for £8.50. These tickets are available to students, senior citizens and unemployed people. This offer is restricted to one ticket per applicant on production of appropriate identification.

The theatre is in Bray's Lane, London WC2 and is close to both Trafalgar Square and Charing Cross tube stations. It can also be reached by buses 1, 24, 29 and 176.

Thank you for calling.

SECTION C   The Translator

You will hear a radio programme in which a translator is being interviewed about her job. For questions 22–27, indicate the most appropriate response, A, B, C or D.   You will hear the recording twice.

Interviewer: In this day and age more and more people learn foreign languages but this has not reduced the demand for translators. As more and more nations trade with each other and have greater contact with each other, so more and more translators are required. But what exactly does the job involve, and what are the highs and lows of being a translator? I spoke to Fiona Gibbs, a translator for many years, and first of all I asked her what presents translators with the greatest difficulty.

Fiona: The worst problem, believe it or not, has little to do with language, it has more to do with personality. I'm not talking about nationality, by the way, because my experience is that you can find the same sorts of people anywhere. No, it's what people are like as individuals that causes the real trouble. I mean, take jokes, for example. You can be translating for somebody and they say something that's meant to be funny and you just know the person you translate it to isn't going to find it the least bit funny because they have a totally different sense of humour. The whole thing falls flat and you feel terribly silly translating it.

Interviewer: What made you want to be a translator?

Fiona: Well, of course a fascination for language was the starting point. I mean, from a very early age I had, I suppose, a gift for languages and I realized that I could pick them up pretty quickly. So when I left school there wasn't really much doubt as to what I'd do at university and then for a living. Also, I thought it would be pretty well-paid, that it would enable me to travel and to gain a real understanding of other cultures and that it would give me job satisfaction because I would be helping people who speak different languages to get on together and work together.

Interviewer: And has all that proved to be the case?

Fiona: Well, yes and no. The money side of it certainly hasn't turned out to be totally true (laughs) but at the same time I suppose I can't really complain. I have travelled a lot and that's been quite enjoyable, although it's involved a lot of very hard work too. I've learnt an enormous amount about a variety of cultures and attitudes but I couldn't honestly say that this has led me to a real understanding of them. I mean, sometimes it's true that the more you learn, the less you know! People really aren't at all simple and you soon find out that you can't generalize about nationalities. I would certainly say, though, that I do help people from different countries to work and socialize together and I get a lot of satisfaction out of that.

Interviewer: Give me an example.

Fiona: Well …, let me see … yes, well there was an occasion when I was translating in a business meeting and a problem was clearly beginning to emerge. I was translating for a client in some rather delicate negotiations but the other person clearly didn't like his manner. My client was, to be honest, being rather aggressive and uncooperative and it looked to me as if the other man was going to get up and storm out of the room any minute. So I started to translate my client's words, well, I made them a little bit softer, less direct shall we say. I mean, I translated it all properly – that's my job – but I phrased it slightly more politely than the original and the atmosphere soon improved. By the end they'd reached a compromise they were both happy with and the meeting broke up with them the best of friends.

Interviewer: And what's the worst situation you've been in as a translator?

Fiona: Oh, that's easy. I was translating for two politicians at a conference and the one employing me really detested the other one. I mean, it was obviously a personal dislike. So he started insulting him and I had to translate all these terrible insults – I had no choice, he was the one paying me – it was just awful. I thought there was going to be a fight and I was worried that the other politician might hit me or something because, after all, I was the one actually saying all these terrible things to him. I was pretty glad to get out of that room at the end, I can tell you.

Interviewer: So, all in all, is it a job that you'd recommend?

Fiona: Yes – certainly that kind of thing doesn't happen very often. But it's not as glamorous as some people seem to think. You do travel a lot but it's hard work and you often don't see much of the places you visit. Most of the time I thoroughly enjoy my work but I must admit it can get a bit boring sometimes. Certainly you need to have, as I do, a real feel for languages – it's not enough just to have studied them – and to really like working with them. I certainly can't imagine myself doing anything else.

Interviewer: Thanks very much, Fiona, I've enjoyed talking to you.

SECTION D   Our Town

You will hear extracts of five different people talking about a town.
You will hear the series twice.

Task One lists different people. As you listen, put them in the order in which you hear them by completing the boxes numbered 28–32 with the appropriate letter.

Task Two lists the different topics mentioned by the people speaking in the five extracts. As you listen, put them in the order in which you hear them by completing the boxes numbered 33–37 with the appropriate letter.

Voice 1:   What makes my job more difficult is that they keep asking me where such and such a shop or hotel or street is. I mean, all I'm concerned with is that they pay the correct fare or show me a valid card, and anyway I don't know where half the places they ask me about are. It's not so bad when there aren't many of them but these days we have loads here, so all these questions hold me up quite a bit and of course that holds up all the people behind me.

Voice 2:   I love it here because it's so easy to get around. I mean, I'm not earning so I can't afford to get a car, which means that I rely on the buses. It's great, because if I get fed up with being on the campus all the time with my head stuck in a book, I can just pop out and easily get anywhere, either into the town or to some of the villages just outside it. It's nice to be able to get into the countryside so easily and forget all about lectures for a while.

Voice 3:   I came here a couple of years ago to set up this business and I certainly haven't regretted it. The place is growing all the time and the population's getting younger, which hasn't done me any harm, because a lot of them are keen on sports. Trade has been good in here ever since I opened up. Racquets and track suits are particularly popular and I have to make sure I keep up with demand.

Voice 4:   Obviously I'm pleased, as is my party, with the town's progress and prosperity but we can't just sit back and be complacent. We've got to think about the longer term and take steps now to avoid problems in the future. The main one I foresee is congestion. We need to widen the roads we've got and build new ones, especially to take the pressure off the centre. Otherwise the whole place will grind to a standstill in a few years' time.

Voice 5:   I don't get much chance to get any shopping done during the week but sometimes I do pop out during my lunch break. The good thing about this town is that you can get more or less anything you want in a small area. The new pedestrian-only place is especially good – there are all sorts of stores there – and I go there sometimes just to get a break from the staff room and all that marking I have to do.

That is the end of Section D. There will now be a ten minute pause to allow you to transfer your answers to the separate answer sheet. Be sure to follow the numbering of all the questions. The question papers and answer sheets will then be collected by your supervisor.

TEST 3

*There are four sections to this test – A, B, C and D. You will hear Section B **once** only. All the other parts of the test will be heard twice.*

During the test, there will be a pause before each part to allow you to look through the questions, and other pauses to let you think about your answers. At the end of every pause you will hear this sound. FX

You should write your answers on the question paper. You will have ten minutes at the end to transfer your answers to the separate answer sheet.

The tape will now be stopped. You must ask any questions now, as you will not be allowed to speak during the test.
PAUSE 00'10"

SECTION A   Malawi

You will hear a talk about the country Malawi. For questions 1–12, complete the sentences.

You will hear the recording twice.

Malawi is one of the smaller African nations. Squashed between Tanzania, Mozambique and Zambia, it has no access to the sea. It used to be known as Nyasaland, a name given to it by its colonial rulers late in the 19th century. It didn't become independent from Britain until the 1960s, when it took on its new name, Malawi.

The country is dominated by a huge lake – Lake Malawi –, the length of England. I travelled down it on a ship called *Entendere*, starting at Chilumba in the North. Ahead lay a journey through the heart of Africa which would take at least three days. And with the ship the only form of transport on the lake it was no surprise that it was packed to the brim with all kinds of people and goods.

We passed dozens of little fishing villages with thatched roofs and mud walls and I didn't see any motorboats or cars. With most places not having harbours, the ship's lifeboats were the only way of getting ashore. Up in the North, there is no access to many of the villages by road and the people rely entirely on the ship's twice-weekly visit for all their supplies. For people and mail, it's the only way to enter or leave the outside world. It's a lifeline and its arrival is a big and joyful event.

The vast majority of Malawians have a lifestyle much as they've had for hundreds of years, living in mud and thatched huts, eating what they grow or what they can fish. It's on the shores of the western side of the lake that the work is done and the fish that keep them all alive are brought ashore by hand, just as they have been for centuries. There are no cars in the villages on the shores of the lake, no telephones, and no supply of electricity or running water. Malawi is one of the very few countries in the world without television, so live entertainment is the only form of entertainment, with music and instruments that are home-made.

Life below the water of Lake Malawi is as colourful and varied as life above it. About 1,000 unique species have been discovered in the lake. Many came to light in the 1950s and are stored, still waiting to be logged and classified. After 300 miles on the most beautiful, unpolluted lake I'd ever seen, the ship reached its most southerly point, the port of Monkey Bay. Sadly, it was the end of my journey but within a few hours the *Entendere* had been refuelled and restocked and was heading back up to the lakeside villages that rely so much upon her.

SECTION B   Animal Watch

You will hear the presenter of a programme about animals giving details of a scheme. For questions 13–18, fill in the missing information.

Listen very carefully because you will hear the recording only once.

Presenter: Our next item is for all those of you who are interested not just in seeing or learning about animals but also in doing something to help them. I'm sure that many of you will have been to Finden Zoo and Hanthorn Animal Park but you may not be aware of the wealth of activity that goes on behind the scenes in those places to do with helping rare and endangered species. Beyond both of those institutions, there are all sorts of projects going on which are helping to save animals in the wild. And you too can help.

How? By joining Animal Watch, a new animal conservation membership scheme run jointly by the zoo and the animal park. It is already playing a major role in raising awareness of and money for important wildlife projects, which are undertaken every year. So by joining you'll be lending a hand to help safeguard the future survival of some of the world's rarest animals. For example, because of illegal hunting, there are now fewer than 4,000 black rhinos in Africa, and in conjunction with the Kenya Wildlife Service, Animal Watch is developing a management plan for the future survival of rhinos in Kenya. And Animal Watch is also very involved in returning animals to the wild. With your help, and the help of other members, they'll be able to return many more to the wild in the future.

So, what are the details on joining? Well, membership costs £10 and this fee will not only make a major contribution to animal conservation but also entitle you to all of the following: a membership card giving you free entry to Finden Zoo and Hanthorn Animal Park for a full year; three editions of the magazine *Explorers News*; and special discounts at the Finden Zoo and Hanthorn Animal Park shops.

You can join by picking up an application form at either of the two institutions or you can phone them and you'll be sent one. All you do then is simply fill it in and then return it, together with the membership fee. So, why not join and help animals all over the world?

OK. Next we're going to find out just what happened when our reporter, Linda Flood went to Scandinavia in search of … (fade)

SECTION C   Children's Book Writers

You will hear a radio interview with a husband and wife who write books for children. For questions 19–28, indicate whether the views are expressed in the interview by writing Yes or No in the box provided.

You will hear the piece twice.

Presenter: My guests today are Ben and Carol Morris, husband and wife authors of some of our most successful children's books. Ben, what's it like working at home together? Does it present difficulties and is there a temptation to waste time just chatting?

Ben: No, it works very well. I think it's very important to be able to talk to somebody when you're doing a book, it's important to have somebody there so that you can say "What do you think of this idea? How do you think this drawing is going?" And there's very little lost time because there are two of us.

Presenter: Is it that one of you does the drawings and one of you does the text?

Carol: No, it's not quite as simple as that. We both draw and we both do the text. We do lots of rough drafts – each drawing in a book can sometimes take up to five stages. You'll have your initial idea for your page, and you might have to research something – like on one book we did that's got lots of spacecraft and things – so that they're semi-realistic. So there's lots of drawing that goes into doing each book and we both work on them.

Ben: Each day, each day's very different. Um … Carol's actually been researching a book recently and producing the sketches for a book about cats and um … because she's been involved with that I've been able to finish off another book for the same publisher, which simply requires artwork. So that's how it is today – you come and see us maybe in a month's time, then perhaps we'll both be into the cat book and deciding which drawings, which jokes, which visual jokes can go in.

Presenter: Yes, you mentioned visual jokes there. In actual fact that's quite interesting because your books are very much part of an idea – perhaps you could almost call it a movement – that has taken books for the very young away from the idea of just simply a picture, one line of text, turn over the page, a picture, one line of text. Your books have moved right away from that, haven't they? Is that something you worked out or that just happened?

Ben: I think it's probably because, as a parent, when you start to read books to your children – and certainly some years ago – you'd be reading a book and, er, it would become tedious, there'd be very little in it to, um, keep your attention going and often you'd be jumping pages and the child would say "Oh, you've missed that, go back" and you'd go back and you'd be reading this terrible, repetitive book. And we thought, if there could be books where you could build in another layer to it … So we did a series of books and we had the story running and then we had, we had cartoon characters at the bottom, making fun of the whole thing, commenting on it. And that was almost for ourselves, to sort of keep our interest going and that seems to be the thing that the parents feel. The parents realize that these two little characters are sending the whole thing up and that it's not getting too serious.

Presenter: Do you think that books can be toys?

Carol: Fun. I think that's our overriding drive with the books, to make them fun for children. We don't want them to open a book and get frightened by all the print. We want the children to work their way through each page, find bits and pieces, go back in the book, find a little rhyme or something that they missed, so that they're constantly amused and they don't actually realize that they're reading.

Ben: I think it's about books becoming games. If you can make a book fun … It's to do with the whole concept of a book, isn't it? You can say "book" to some children and it puts them off immediately but if you say it's a toy rather than a book – it's almost as if books have the wrong name – and if a child enjoys playing with a book, the book becomes a game and that makes reading fun.

Presenter: Well, your books are very inventive and very funny. Um, can you keep the jokes coming, are they ever going to run out?

Ben: I hope not.

Carol: I'm sure we have lots more ideas in us yet!

Presenter: Ben and Carol Morris, thanks very much. Next week Jane Smith joins me to look at new fiction for older children … (fade)

SECTION D   Recent Purchases

You will hear extracts of five different people talking about things they have recently bought.

You will hear the series twice.

TASK ONE Letters A–H list different items. As you listen, put them in the order in which you hear them being talked about by completing the boxes numbered 29–33 with the appropriate letter.

TASK TWO Letters A–H list the different opinions expressed by the people speaking in the five extracts. As you listen, put them in the order in which you hear them by completing the boxes numbered 34–38 with the appropriate letter.

Voice 1: … yes, well they came round and delivered it last week – they had awful trouble getting it through the door and up the stairs – and they fitted it in in no time at all. It wasn't all that difficult to work out how to use it – there's a manual that explains all the switches and dials and buttons. It cost quite a bit, but then it isn't just your average model and I'm certainly not expecting to have to replace it for ages – I mean, it's on a long guarantee and it's not the sort of thing you get all that often, is it? It's so handy having it – none of that endless scrubbing any more. I just can't imagine how I ever managed without it. Anyway, I'll have to go. The sheets are probably done by now and I'll have to hang them out.

Voice 2: I had a bit of trouble with the reception when I first got it – the sound was rather muffled and sometimes there was, like, a shadow on the screen but I've had them round to look at it and apparently it was something to do with the tuning and they sorted that out. I chose the make mostly because of the design – I mean, some of them can be really ugly and take up far too much space, don't you think? I guess it's a question of taste but I like the shape of it and it fits in well with everything else. Of course, since I bought it I've seen it advertised much cheaper somewhere else but that always happens, doesn't it?

Voice 3: It might not be the prettiest thing in the world but it does the job OK and that's all I really care about. The last one I had was really old and it wasn't picking things up very well so I thought it was about time I splashed out on a new one. It's got this special attachment for getting dust and bits out of difficult places, which the other one didn't have and it's got a very long lead, so you don't have to keep taking it out and plugging it in again. The only trouble is, it makes the most dreadful racket – I mean, when you've got it switched on you can hardly hear yourself think!

Voice 4:   Well, you know, everyone says how useful they are so I thought I'd better get one, but to be honest I still can't see how it makes anything better for me. I thought I'd never be able to sort out how it works – these complicated modern things aren't my strong point, you know – but that hasn't been the case. No, it's just that it can do all these things I don't need. I mean, apart from anything else, my finances are hardly that complex and I have no particular desire to work out what they're going to be for years to come. Mind you, one thing's for sure. Now I've bought it, I'm going to be broke for ages. I wish I hadn't bothered.

Voice 5:   I thought I'd worked everything out just right when I ordered it but when it arrived I realized that it didn't quite fit where I was going to put it so I've just had to put it where there's enough room for it, which is by no means satisfactory. Apart from that, though, there's nothing wrong with it. You can defrost things in it – I couldn't do that with the last one –, there's plenty of space in it and it's easy to clean. It takes a bit longer than the last one to heat up when you switch it on but I've got used to that and everything I've done in it so far has come out just right – you set the timer and when it makes this sort of 'beep' noise, you know that whatever you've got in there is ready.

That is the end of Section D. There will now be a ten minute pause to allow you to transfer your answers to the separate answer sheet. Be sure to follow the numbering of all the questions. The question papers and answer sheets will then be collected by your supervisor.

TEST 4

*There are four sections to this test – A, B, C and D. You will hear Section B **once** only. All the other parts of the test will be heard twice.*

During the test, there will be a pause before each part to allow you to look through the questions, and other pauses to let you think about your answers. At the end of every pause you will hear this sound. FX

You should write your answers on the question paper. You will have ten minutes at the end to transfer your answers to the separate answer sheet.

The tape will now be stopped. You must ask any questions now, as you will not be allowed to speak during the test. PAUSE 00'10"

SECTION A   The Ring-Pull Can
You will hear part of a talk about the ring-pull can, the container in which many drinks are sold. For questions 1–12, complete the sentences.   You will hear the recording twice.

A burglar alarm, a parachute, a crash barrier, a smoke alarm. These machines and many others wait to work. And when they are required to work, they have to work once, perfectly.

Among the most precise of these patiently waiting devices is the ring-pull can. The ring-pull can is a pressurized container used both to transport and to store, perhaps for long periods of time, a commercially sold drink. This type of can owes its popularity to the fact that it's totally safe, it's economical, it's easy to open, it doesn't leak and it's not damaging to the environment. Four thousand of these cans are opened every second worldwide.

Success depends upon the ring-pull mechanism working every time. The entire product is based on a small cut in the can. Far from being a simple matter, it is an engineering masterpiece. The surface of the can is 0.28 millimetres thick. The cut is less than half that, being 0.09 millimetres deep, about the thickness of the average banknote. When the can is manufactured, the cut that is made in the metal where it is to be opened changes the physical condition of the metal so that it can withstand high internal pressure but also break very cleanly and very easily.

The market requires reliability. Reliability means a clean break every time a can is opened. And a clean break is dependent on the size and shape of the cut in the can. This has been developed by working out how not to make it – negative engineering. If the cut is too shallow, the top is difficult to open and if it's too deep the can could leak. If the cut had a V-shape, it would break with uneven, sharp edges. If it had a square shape, the can might burst when it is opened.

The depth of the cut in the metal is varied so that when the top is pulled open, there is a two-stage action. At the point where the top is pulled, the cut is relatively deep and the metal is very thin and so it breaks easily. However, the top is only allowed to move a short distance before it is stopped by a thickening of the metal where the cut is shallower. This hesitation allows the can to release pressure, which ensures that you don't pour the contents over your neighbour. Additional pressure on the top is then required to complete the opening.

The ring-pull top must open every time. A significant failure rate would be a commercial disaster. And yet it has to be manufactured for just over a penny to a precision similar to that of a Swiss watch worth hundreds of thousands of pounds.

SECTION B   What's on this Weekend

You will hear part of a radio programme, in which future events are discussed. For questions 13–20, indicate whether the statements are made about each event by writing Yes or No in the box provided.

Listen very carefully because you will hear the recording only once.

Presenter: …I'm Charles Jordan, with you until 4 o'clock every afternoon this week and every week, Monday to Friday. As usual, I'm joined today by Clare Fielding to talk about what's on in and around the city this weekend. Clare, I suppose the big event this weekend is the Highfield Carnival …

Clare: Yes, that's certainly the obvious suggestion for anybody who's looking for something to do in the city this weekend. It has, er, become a huge event and there'll be an estimated 600,000 people heading for it, so take some sensible advice and perhaps leave the car at home. And, um, get there early on in the day, I would say, rather than leaving it till later. The carnival is on Sunday and Monday and there should be plenty to do for people of all ages.

Presenter: I know a lot of the locals there complain that it started very much as a local festival and now it's been taken over and they've lost control of it.

Clare: Yes, to a certain extent outsiders have come in, but, I mean, it's inevitable that if you're going to have an internationally recognized street festival, then, you know, it can't just be a small community-based event as well. And I think it's fun and it still has a really good sense of local colour.

Presenter: So, what else is on?

Clare: Well, we've got the Frankton rock festival as well this weekend, which is our longest-running open-air festival, having survived all these years. I suppose the real highlight for fans will be the appearance of *The Dogs*, who have really taken the music business by storm. They've got a big following. The other bands on over the weekend include a good cross-section, such as *The Upsetters* and *The Intense* …

Presenter: (laughs) A lot of people I haven't heard of. Is there anything on I have heard of?

Clare: Well, let's see, er, a new production of the modern opera *Nighttime* is due to open at the Opera House on Friday. This should be a great production, er, you know, it's a great spectacle to watch. I think opera has started to have a wider appeal to a mass audience now. Ticket sales are up and I think it's going to stay that way.

Presenter: OK, well thanks Clare. We'll take a break now and then we'll be back to talk some more about some of the things we can do this weekend … (fade)

SECTION C   The Explorer

You will hear part of an interview with an explorer. For questions 21–30, complete the sentences.

You will hear the piece twice.

Announcer: … and our next news bulletin will be in half an hour at 3 o'clock.

Interviewer: Welcome back to the programme, where my guest today is Ranulph Fiennes, the explorer. We've been talking about the first two trips you made. You must have been accused on both those trips, and on all the subsequent ones, of putting the lives of others in danger. You're obviously very conscious that you need a back-up team and that you're responsible for others. Do you think you've taken a lot of unnecessary risks?

Explorer: We spend a lot of time planning to avoid the risks, because the risks are liable to cause you to fail, but of my expeditions over the last five years, apart from the one I've just come back from, they've all been what technically could be described as failures. However, they haven't killed anybody. I mean, next year maybe somebody will die but so far, in 22 years of expeditions nobody's died and that's, um, over hundreds of thousands of miles of very remote areas, so the planning must have been reasonably good and in terms of the risk factor I think we foresaw them sufficiently to get the right equipment and the right training so that we didn't get deaths en route.

Interviewer: Is it that the whole point is just to do it rather than to come up with some sort of scientific conclusion or to prove something that would interest the physicists?

Explorer: If you take, for example, the expedition which we'll be setting out on next November, that expedition has three aims. On that expedition, in Antarctica, we've been set a target that we must raise enough money to complete building a disease research centre. Now last year in Siberia we raised, with the help of all the people who sponsored us at a penny a mile of our progress, £1.3m. Well that was a 480-mile journey, next year it's 1800 miles, so at a penny a mile we should raise £4.5m, which together with last year's bit will be over £5m to build the centre. So the charitable side of the expedition is one of the sides. The scientific side, which has been going on, the same scientific work for the last five expeditions, is coming to a head on this particular expedition. It's studying how much the human body can put up with when it's working extremely hard in extreme temperatures but is not eating enough food. This is something which is of great interest to nutritionists and all sorts of other doctors and military people and so on and so forth. Next year the expedition team will consist of 6 people, only two of them actually on the travel team, the other four are scientists with a wealth of heavy equipment which has to be taken to the edge of the Antarctic so that the team members can be subjected to all the tests the day before they leave and the two days after they come back. It's no good if they eat anything when they come back famished having lost 4 stone, before they go for all the tests. The scientific side, like the charity side, is vital. And then of course there is the physical challenge side, which to most armchair sceptics is something which can very easily be laughed at and therefore we don't stress it any more. In the old days, say 40 or 50 years ago, this was in itself sufficient.

Interviewer: Is there any one achievement you've not yet got under your belt that's still on the horizon? You haven't, I know, been to a Pole unaccompanied or unsupported – in other words without the help of dogs and without the help of machinery.

Explorer: Yes, I've been to both Poles and, um, so that's that, but in terms of getting to either one of them without support, um, we hope to get to the South Pole and back this year and then in future years we'll think again about the North. Next year's goal, in Antarctica, is to complete what is a very testing journey, particularly in terms of planning – how the sledges that we have to pull should be designed and how to take maximum calories with minimum weight. Last time I felt that we just didn't have enough food and it was a very unpleasant experience slowly starving whilst continually trying to move forward through the cold. This time we've upped the number of calories but now we've got to keep going for 100 days on what we carry on day one – that's in terms of fuel and food.

Interviewer: Well, the best of luck with that and all your other expeditions …

Explorer: Thank you.

Interviewer: And thanks for talking to me today. My guest was Ranulph Fiennes … (fade)

SECTION D Talking About Other People

You will hear extracts of five different people talking about other people.

You will hear the series twice.

TASK ONE Letters A–H list people being talked about. As you listen, put them in the order in which you hear them by completing the boxes numbered 31–35 with the appropriate letter.

TASK TWO Letters A–H list descriptions of the people mentioned in the five extracts. As you listen, put them in the order in which you hear them by completing the boxes numbered 36–40 with the appropriate letter.

Voice 1: To be honest I still don't know whether he took me for a ride. I mean, I took the thing in for a service and he talked about this and that fault when I thought it was basically running pretty well. Well, I had no way of knowing whether he was being straight with me or not because I don't know the first thing about it. I just had to take his word for it, what else could I do? If I'd told him I wasn't satisfied and taken it somewhere else, who's to say it would have been any better?

Voice 2: I wasn't very keen on the way he treated me, to say the least. I mean, all I did was make a minor complaint about how long my order was taking and he just turned round and said; ''Well if that's how you feel about it, why don't you go somewhere else? Can't you see I'm dealing with other people's bills?'' Well, I can understand they get rushed off their feet at the busy times but I don't think that justifies being so bad-mannered. And when it finally did come and he was serving it out, you should have seen the nasty look he gave me! Charming, I thought.

Voice 3: He certainly doesn't give a very good impression to customers, if my experience is anything to go by. I mean, I phoned up to make a simple booking and I said exactly what I wanted but he didn't sound as though he was paying attention and then he got it all wrong. When I got back to him and pointed this out he said he'd sort it all out straight away but then I didn't hear anything for ages. I checked and it turned out that he'd forgotten all about it. Honestly! Well, all I can say is I wouldn't recommend staying there if that's how the staff operate.

Voice 4: It wasn't as if I was asking for anything particularly tricky. All I was asking was for him to change it or give me a refund – I had the receipt – but he looked at me as if I'd asked him for something totally impossible. I mean, at first I thought he was pretending not to know what I was talking about just to be awkward but he really was as thick as he seemed! Well, I spelt it all out for him and eventually he just about got it and went off and got me another one. But really, you'd think a store like that could employ people a bit brighter than that.

Voice 5: Well, I kept trying to make arrangements with him but he was never there when he was supposed to be. I mean, the job only needed a bit of finishing off – a bit of drilling here, a few nails there – but I could never get hold of him and the whole thing dragged on far longer than it should have done. And when I did get in touch with him, we fixed up a time but he didn't keep it. I'm not saying he was no good – there was nothing wrong with the quality of what he did – it's just that I never knew whether he was going to turn up when he said he would or not.

That is the end of Section D. There will now be a ten minute pause to allow you to transfer your answers to the separate answer sheet. Be sure to follow the numbering of all the questions. The question papers and answer sheets will then be collected by your supervisor.

TEST 5

*There are four sections to this test – A, B, C and D. You will hear Section B **once** only. All the other parts of the test will be heard twice.*

During the test, there will be a pause before each part to allow you to look through the questions, and other pauses to let you think about your answers. At the end of every pause you will hear this sound. FX

You should write your answers on the question paper. You will have ten minutes at the end to transfer your answers to the separate answer sheet.

The tape will now be stopped. You must ask any questions now, as you will not be allowed to speak during the test. PAUSE 00'10"

SECTION A   Wildlife on Golf Courses
You will hear a talk about the wildlife found on golf courses. For questions 1–10, complete the sentences.

You will hear the recording twice.

Golf today is one of the fastest growing sports. There are now almost two and a half thousand courses in Britain and that number is increasing each year. With a growing number of people wanting to take up the game, more and more clubs are being formed to meet demand. All over the country, new courses are being constructed on farmland no longer needed for that purpose because of the increased efficiency of modern agricultural methods. Yet it's not just the golfers who are benefiting from this rapid expansion. Many of the courses provide a haven for wildlife and most of the new courses under construction have been planned carefully to ensure that this will always be so. With proper planning, the land used in developing these new courses not only provides much needed new playing facilities, it also creates an environment in which the natural wildlife can flourish.

While some forms of wildlife on courses are positively encouraged, there are, however, a few animals that can only be regarded as a nuisance. Moles love golf courses and they thrive on them. But as they surface, they push up piles of earth above the grass that do considerable damage to the playing surface. Encouraging wildlife onto a golf course can prove counter-productive. What can you do if a magpie removes your ball from the hole and flies away with it?

But the vast majority of wildlife on a golf course helps maintain nature's natural balance and in addition provides an attractive and interesting backdrop to the game. The ponds and lakes, for example, attract a large variety of plant and animal life and it's surprising how quickly life appears in and around a newly created body of water. And the large variety of habitats that are often found on a course make finding food a little easier for the birds.

At many coastal golf courses adders can often be found. They don't present a threat to the golfers, as they are shy, timid snakes that glide off into the undergrowth if disturbed. Since they feed mainly on rodents, they play an important role in controlling the number of mice and other creatures that do damage to golf courses.

Some inhabitants of the golf course are easily overlooked and only noticed when your ball lands close by, but you wouldn't want to get too close to the wood ants – they have a formidable bite and a painful sting.

It may come as some surprise to learn that rabbits, probably the biggest natural pests on a golf course, may have been a direct inspiration for the game in the first place, since it is said that golf was first played by Scottish shepherds hitting small stones into rabbit holes. This doesn't, however, excuse them for digging up carefully looked-after playing surfaces.

And so there's little doubt that, as well as the enjoyment golfers receive from the game itself, golf is helping to provide a much-needed sanctuary for wildlife.

SECTION B   Writing Competition
You will hear the presenter of a radio programme about books giving details of a competition. For questions 11–17, fill in the missing information.

Listen very carefully because you will hear the recording only once.

Presenter: … and that's nearly the end of today's programme except to give you, as I promised at the beginning, the details of our writing competition. As you may recall, we launched our short story competition last year and the overwhelming response, together with the high standard of entries, has prompted us to hold it again this year. The competition is again being organized in conjunction with *Your World* magazine.

Your story can be on any subject and must not be more than 2,500 words long. Entrants may submit one story only and it must be typed and double-spaced on one side of the paper only. Please note that entries will not be returned so we suggest that you send in a clear copy of your story and keep the original. Entries must arrive by March 27th and when you send it, include a postcard containing your name, address and postcode, and a daytime telephone number.

The panel of judges includes Elizabeth Grant, the editor of *Your World* and Graham Gower, the successful novelist, whose latest book, *Waste of Time*, has just been published. The third judge is Mark Robinson, who gave up a high-powered job as a TV executive to write plays for television, several of which have been critically acclaimed. The winners will be announced on this programme in early May and then, in July, the winning story will be read on this programme and published in *Your World*. In addition to publication and broadcast, the first prize is a *Wordsmith* word processor, worth over £700. Two second-prize winners will each receive a *High Style* word processor worth over £400 and a special prize of £100, donated by Graham Gower, will go to the entry which shows most originality.

So, why not see if you can write a winning story and then see it in print and hear it on the air, as well as winning wonderful prizes? Send your entries to the usual address:- *The Book Show*, KP Radio, 13, Waterfall Place, Birmingham B3 6TF.

So, until the same time next week, goodbye.

SECTION C   Making Complaints

You will hear part of a radio programme about making complaints. For questions 18–27, complete the sentences.

You will hear the piece twice.

Presenter: Right, in this part of the show I'm going to be talking about complaining – how to make proper complaints about shoddy goods and services and how best to get things sorted out – and I have with me Joan Brand, the head of the Consumer Services Department and Alan Flynn, principal lawyer for the Consumers Association. We'll be taking your calls, so if you want advice about a complaint, a reminder of our number – 071-973 9733. Alan, are lots of complaints settled very quickly these days? Do people say, "OK, yes, I surrender, you're absolutely right" or is there naturally a kind of wish to defend themselves and deflect complaints?

Alan: It depends upon the company you're involved with. I think if it's a good company that's bothered about its reputation, then they're aware that it's good public relations to get complaints sorted out quickly.

Presenter: And who do you complain to, and how?

Alan: Well if you've got a complaint against a shop for instance, then there's often very little point in complaining to the assistant, they simply haven't got the authority to sort your complaint out. So ask to speak to the manager. If the manager's not there, then make sure you fix an appointment to see him. In many cases that sort of face-to-face contact can sort things out. Or telephone the manager the next day. Go to the right sort of person in the organization who has the authority to deal with complaints.

Presenter: Joan, you'd back that up would you?

Joan: Yes, I think it's important that the first thing you do when you go to the trader is to make sure you're talking to the right person. And go to the trader as soon as possible to put your case because if you delay it unreasonably you can create problems later on.

Presenter: I wonder perhaps if you could give us a typical case history, if there is such a thing.

Alan: Well one of the complaints that we come across often at this time of year are people who've gone away on holiday and they've found that the service that's been provided isn't what they expected. The hotel's nowhere near the beach, for instance and it says in the brochure that it's only 200 metres down the road …

Presenter: We've all had that.

Alan: … we've all come across that sort of problem. What we also come across however, is that people then decide to complain when they come home. Well obviously, that's silly. If you've got a complaint, talk to the representative on the spot and with any luck you can have your holiday problems sorted out there and then. If, however, that doesn't work, come back, write to the tour operator, ask for compensation and if they fob you off with a feeble excuse then be persistent, write again, and if you think you've got a case, then think about taking it to court.

Presenter: Do you require a lot of determination and endurance?

Joan: You can do. Again, it depends upon the company concerned. Um, but um, there are circumstances, perhaps with some large companies, where there seem to be lots and lots of barriers between you making your complaint and then getting through to somebody to sort it out.

Presenter: And a case history from you? What is one that you remember particularly?

Joan: Um … perhaps somebody purchasing a pair of shoes, for example, and getting them home and perhaps wearing them once and the heel falling off or some fault appearing and then going back to the shop and being told "It's nothing to do with us, you've got to send them back to the manufacturer."

Presenter: Well, what rights do we have? I mean, what constraints are there on manufacturers, do they have to observe particular rules?

Joan: The basic rights by law actually lie with the shop and when you purchase anything from one there are three rights that the law gives you. First, the goods have got to be properly described. Secondly, the goods have got to be of a saleable quality …

Presenter: And they've got to do what they're supposed to do, haven't they?

Joan: … yes and, er, additionally, if you say to a retailer that you want a product to do a particular thing, for a particular purpose, it's got to be fit for that purpose.

Presenter: OK, that's the subject launched and I know that the calls are coming in – we're just sorting you out into some sort of order –, so we'll take a break now and we'll be back in a minute…

SECTION D   Buildings

You will hear five extracts of different people talking about buildings.

You will hear the series twice.

TASK ONE Letters A–H list buildings. As you listen, put them in the order in which you hear them being talked about by completing the boxes numbered 28–32 with the appropriate letter.

TASK TWO Letters A–H list different opinions of the buildings expressed by the people speaking in the five extracts. As you listen, put them in the order in which you hear them by completing the boxes numbered 33–37 with the appropriate letter.

Voice 1: Well, I know a lot of people rave about how remarkable the design of the place is but quite frankly I don't think much of it. I mean, once you're in it you could wander about for hours without ever knowing where you are or where you're going. OK, it may be the very latest thing but you try and find your way around it! I went there once for a meeting and it took me ages to find the room I was looking for – all the corridors look exactly the same and I didn't see any list of all the firms who have space there.

Voice 2: It's a huge building and all that and there's no denying that the town needed it but it has its drawbacks. It took me ages to find a toilet when I went to see something that was on in the Main Hall there and they don't seem to have made much provision for the disabled, which caused us some trouble because I was there with a friend in a wheelchair. I think they should have put a bit more thought into the planning of it and considered the needs of everyone. Still, there are so many things going on there all the time that we certainly can't complain any more that there's a lack of entertainment in this town.

Voice 3: It's terribly convenient for me. I mean, I can see it from my living room window, and all I have to do is pop out and I can pick up everything I need, virtually on my doorstep. Having said that, though, I don't think it was a very good idea to put it there. I mean, it clashes with everything else so much. There's this whole row of buildings that have been there for ages and that we're all used to and then there's this new thing, sticking out like a sore thumb. Like I say, I don't mind it as a building, I'd just sooner it wasn't *there*.

Voice 4: A lot of people have said that it's the best-looking building in town and I must say that I'm inclined to agree. Not that there's a lot to compare it with in this town! Still, it certainly looks most impressive when it's all lit up at night and they say it's attracting a lot more people to the area. I haven't actually been in but I know someone who's stayed there and they say the rooms are on a rather grand scale and the part where they hold conferences and other functions is rather splendid.

Voice 5: The route there isn't very well signposted, which is a serious mistake in my view – you'd think they'd make sure that people had no trouble getting there. I mean it's not exactly close to anywhere else – it's in a rather out of the way place – so that's really important. There aren't enough trains into town from it either, I gather. And there isn't very much information in the place, which is awful. I mean, there's nothing worse if you've just touched down in a strange place than not knowing what to do or where to go once you've arrived. They made such a fuss about building it and how much good it would do to the town, you'd have thought they'd have made an effort to make sure the people who use it get a good impression.

That is the end of Section D. There will now be a ten minute pause to allow you to transfer your answers to the separate answer sheet. Be sure to follow the numbering of all the questions. The question papers and answer sheets will then be collected by your supervisor.

SAMPLE STUDENT ANSWERS FOR PAPER 2 SECTION A

The student answers below and on pages 175–176 are genuine answers and are therefore not flawless, although they demonstrate good task achievement.

TEST 1 SECTION A

Dear Sir/Madam,

I have just returned from my holiday on Atlantic Island and I feel thoroughly disappointed and annoyed because it was totally different than what I was led to expect.

When I went to book my holiday in your agency they assured me that the place was environmentally protected and that the water was clean and pure. I was convinced that the place where I was going was the most beautiful and clean place I could choose. By the time I got there I realized that the brochures I saw and the information they gave me were all wrong. The place was completely dirty and the sea-water was polluted. Even though I tried to enjoy myself as much as I could, by the second day I was suffering from a terrible sore throat. After all this – I was so upset because of the way I had wasted my money.

A week after I came back home, I found a report on the condition of Atlantic Island beaches that I wished I had seen before. This report shows the change in the situation of the beaches in the last three years. Now there is only half the number of safe swimming beaches that there used to be. The amount of heavily polluted water is now double. In conclusion, it's getting worse every year.

I think something ought to be done so no more tourists get a wrong idea of the place.

As you will realize, we are completely disgusted with the holiday your company provided. I trust you will agree that at least I deserve a substantial refund of my money. If not I shall have to take matters a step further.

Yours faithfully,

Lorena Mendoza

TEST 2 SECTION A

I received six entrants from six different schools giving the ideas for the best way of teaching English. I, as a judge, read all of them carefully and without any predjudices.

I'd like to repeat the main aim of our competition which was to find how to make all the children enthusiastic learners of English. All the entrants give some ideas on teaching English, but I think that something was missed in most of them. There is nothing said about the result of using a specific idea and about the children's response to it. The only exception is the entry marked with T.P. initials. It gives information about children's attitude to writing letters in English and receiving these that's why I estimate it as the best one.

I also like the ideas of teaching English described in S.F. and K.K's entries. As to me, a personal contact with native speakers is the best, the most interesting and the most efficient way of teaching any foreign language. It takes place during the holidays, which gives possibilities of using unusual methods of teaching supported by everyday practise.

What I like in K.K's entry is the motto "Little and Often" because that idea of teaching doesn't let children get bored.

The idea of running an English club given in A.C's entry could be, in my opinion, more useful for older children or students even. But I cannot deny that activities like watching films or taking part in language competitions can be helpful.

A.G. and P.C's ideas can bring a little of practical use and fun to the lessons but honestly they don't really show the new points of teaching languages.

Summing up, I am glad to find some enthusiastic teachers who wanted to share their opinions and experiences with us.

Magdalene Zacikiewicz

TEST 3 SECTION A

Letter a

Dear Prof. M. Pearce,

I am writing to you in response to your letter cancelling your lecture.

I am grateful to you for providing me with a prompt notice which enables me to find a suitable substitute for you.

I also want to express my concern about your indisposition and my best wishes for your recovery.

Yours sincerely,
A. Bauer

Letter b

Dear Richard,

Thanks for your letter which arrived at my office while I was on holiday.

It was nice to hear from you after such a long time and I am desperately looking forward to meeting you on Oct. 5th. Fortunately, I've got a guest-room at my place which you are welcome to use for as long as it suits you.

At the moment I'm busy organizing the programme for the autumn course at the institute. We invited Prof. Pearce to speak about British travellers in the U.S.A. in the nineteenth century, but she had to cancel her appearance on her doctor's advice. It seems to me a lucky coincidence that your business brings you here now. I want to use this stroke of luck to ask you a big favour. Can't you stand in for her and give a lecture on the evening of October 6th? The subject area must generally be on the English–American relationship. Your presentation should be reinforced by illustrations. Please think over the matter and let me know your decision a.s.a.p. You'd help me a lot, if you said yes.

Despite this, I'm looking forward to seeing you in October.

Best wishes,
Andrea

TEST 4 SECTION A

The Editor
XXX XXXX
XXX XXXX

Dear Sir/Madam,

I would like to respond to the letter written by Mr Gerald Bell which appeared in your newspaper the 16th of October.

I was most upset when I read his opinions. Since I was included in the delegation from Sweden that was visiting your area in the beginning of October, I can clarify some main points which Mr Bell seems to have misunderstood.

Firstly I would like to emphasize the importance of these type of contacts between similar regions in different countries. It can result in a lot of useful relationships between industries and business.

During our visit we visited colleges and schools, where we discussed the students' problems and their ideas how to solve them.

Furthermore we visited some local business and industries, which was very interesting. We were also invited to some worthwile lectures about subjects like tourism, travel and education.

This is just the beginning of a long, fruitful and interesting cooperation between two small areas in England and Sweden. We all know that we can not change the world but hopefully we can make life much easier in our regions.

The main reason why we are doing this is to help industries and local business to survive in these hard times. It is very sad that people like Mr Bell don't understand that through helping local business we help the inhabitants of the area as well.

Finally, I would like to assure Mr Bell that the Swedish Government paid for all expenses.

Yours faithfully,

Cecilia Åkerdahl

TEST 5 SECTION A

Letter a

Dear Mrs Milne,

It was a pleasure to hear from you after such a long time. I see that news travels fast.

It was very kind of you to ask me to stay with you during the holiday, and to have taken the trouble to find some information about a course. But unfortunately I have just booked a sports holiday with Southern Star Holidays. They also offer an English language tuition classes in the morning. That would really be ideal for me as it would allow me to have my afternoon to relax.

I am still waiting for a reply from Southern Star Holidays and if for any reason I could not get a booking I would be delighted to take up your offer, that is if you will still have me!!

All my family send their love to Vicky, Jenny, Roy and yourself.

Love,

Marie-Ange

PS Thanks again for your offer, keep in touch.

Letter b

Dear Sir/Madam,

Having just read your advertisement regarding the sports holiday in New Zealand's South Island, I would be grateful if you could send me a detailed list of all the sports facilities you provide, as well as the equipment required, or equipment hire price.

Could you please forward some information concerning the cost of inexpensive accommodation as I am a student and have a limited budget.

I am also very interested in taking English language classes and would like further details about the cost, and also the level of the classes provided.

Many thanks in advance.

Yours sincerely,

Marie-Ange Jean Baptiste